OUT & ABOUT

• WALKING GUIDES TO BRITAIN •

No 10

The West Country

First published in Great Britain in 1996 by
Marshall Cavendish Books, London
(a division of Marshall Cavendish Partworks Ltd)

Copyright © 1996 Marshall Cavendish

All maps in this publication are reproduced from Ordnance Survey 1:25,000 maps with the permission of
The Controller of Her Majesty's Stationery Office, © Crown copyright.

ISBN 0319 00746 4

British Library Cataloguing in Publication Data:
A catalogue record for this book is available from the British Library

Printed and bound in Malaysia

Some of this material has previously appeared in the Marshall Cavendish partwork OUT & ABOUT

While every effort has been made to check the accuracy of these walks, neither Marshall Cavendish nor Ordnance Survey can be held responsible for any errors or omissions, nor for any consequences arising from the use of information contained in this book. Marshall Cavendish welcomes readers' letters pointing out changes that have taken place in land ownership, access, etc., or inaccuracies in the walks' routes or descriptions.

CONTENTS

Introduction to

OUT & ABOUT

• WALKING GUIDES TO BRITAIN •

Walking has become one of the most popular pastimes in Britain. To enjoy walking, you don't need any special skills, you don't have to follow rules or join expensive clubs, and you don't need any special equipment – though a pair of walking boots is a good idea! It is an easy way of relaxing and getting some exercise, and of enjoying nature and the changing seasons.

The OUT & ABOUT WALKING GUIDES TO BRITAIN will give you ideas for walks in your own neighbourhood and in other areas of Britain. All the walks are devised around a theme and range in length from about 2 to 9 miles (3.25 to 14.5 km) and in difficulty from very easy to mildly strenuous. Since each walk is circular, you will always be able to get back to your starting point.

Devised by experts and tested for accuracy, all the walks are accompanied by clear, practical instructions and an enlarged section of the relevant Ordnance Survey map. The flavour of the walk and highlights to look out for are described in the introductory text.

LOCAL COLOUR

Background features give you extra insight into items of local interest. The OUT & ABOUT WALKING GUIDES TO BRITAIN relate legends, point out unusual architectural details, provide a potted history of the lives of famous writers and artists connected with a particular place, explain traditional crafts still practised by local artisans, and uncover the secrets behind an ever-changing landscape.

DISCOVER NATURE

One of the greatest pleasures in going for a walk is the sense of being close to nature. On the walks suggested in the OUT & ABOUT WALKING GUIDES TO BRITAIN, you can feel the wind, smell the pine trees, hear the birds and see the beauty of the countryside. You will become more aware of the seasons – the life cycles of butterflies, the mating calls of birds, the protective behaviour of all creatures with their young. You will see the beginning of new life in the forests and fields, the bluebell carpets in spring woodlands, the dazzling beauty of rhododendron bushes in early summer, the swaying cornfields of summer and the golden colours of leaves in autumn. The OUT & ABOUT WALKING GUIDES TO BRITAIN tell you what to look out for and where to find it.

NATURE WALK

Occasional nature walk panels will highlight an interesting feature that you will see on your walk. You will learn about natural and manmade details in the landscape, how to tell which animal or bird has nibbled the cones in a pine forest, what nurse trees are and what a triangulation point is.

FACT FILE

The fact file will give you at-a-glance information about each walk to help you make your selection.

* **general location**

os **map reference for Ordnance Survey map with grid reference for starting point**

miles 0 1 2 3 4 5 6 7 8 9
kms 0 1 2 3 4 5 6 7 8 9 10 11 12 13 14 15
length of the walk in miles and kilometres

* **time needed if walking at an average speed**

* **character of the walk: easy/easy with strenuous parts/mildly strenuous; hills to be climbed and muddy or dangerous areas are pointed out**

P **parking facilities near the start of the walk**

T **public transport information**

* **facilities for refreshment, including pubs serving lunchtime meals, restaurants, tea rooms and picnic areas**

WC **location of toilets**

* **historic sites**

ORDNANCE SURVEY MAPS

All the walks in the OUT & ABOUT WALKING GUIDES TO BRITAIN are illustrated on large-scale, full-colour maps supplied by the Ordnance Survey. Ordnance Survey are justifiably proud of their worldwide reputation for excellence and accuracy. For extra clarity, the maps have been enlarged to a scale of 1:21,120 (3 inches to 1 mile).

The route for each walk is marked clearly on the map with a broken red line, and the numbers along the

ABOVE: *Colourful narrowboats are always an attractive feature on inland waterways.*

route refer you to the numbered stages in the written directions. In addition, points of interest are marked on the maps with letters. Each one is mentioned in the walk directions and is described in detail in the introductory text.

COUNTRYWISE

The countryside is one of our greatest resources. If we treat it with respect, we can preserve it for the future.

Throughout the countryside there is a network of paths and byways. Some are former trading routes, others are simply the paths villagers took to visit one another in the days before public transport. Most are designated 'rights of way': foot-paths, open only to people on foot, and bridleways, open to people on foot, horseback or bicycle. These paths can be identified on Ordnance Survey maps and verified, in cases of dispute, by the definitive map for the area, held by the relevant local authority.

THE LAW OF TRESPASS

If you find a public right of way barred to you, you may remove the obstruction or take a short detour around it. However, in England and Wales, if you stray from the footpath you are trespassing and could be sued in a civil court for damages. In Scotland, rights of way are not recorded on definitive maps, nor is there a law of trespass. Although you may cross mountain and moorland paths, landowners are permitted to impose restrictions on access, such as during the grouse-shooting season, which should be obeyed.

If you are following a public right of way and find, for example, that your path is blocked by a field of crops, you are entitled to walk the line of the footpath through the crops, in single file. Farmers are required, by law, to restore public rights of way within 14 days of ploughing. However, if you feel uncomfortable about doing this and can find a way round, then do so. But report the matter to the local authority who will take the necessary action to clear the correct route.

RIGHT: *The stunning patchwork of fields surrounding the picturesque village of Widecombe in the heart of Dartmoor makes a beautiful setting for the famous annual fair.*
BELOW: *Brown hares boxing in spring are a fascinating sight.*

It is illegal for farmers to place a bull on its own in a field crossed by a right of way (unless the bull is not a recognized dairy breed). If you come across a bull alone in a field, find another way round.

COMMONS AND PARKS

There are certain areas in England and Wales where you may be able to wander without keeping to paths, such as most commons and beaches. There are also country parks, set up by local authorities for public recreation – parkland, woodland, heath or farmland.

The National Trust is the largest private landowner in England and Wales. Its purpose is to preserve areas of natural beauty and sites of historic interest by acquisition, holding them in trust for public access and enjoyment. Information on access may be obtained from National Trust headquarters at

THE COUNTRY CODE

■ **Enjoy the countryside, and respect its life and work**

■ **Always guard against risk of fire**

■ **Fasten all gates**

■ **Keep your dogs under close control**

■ **Keep to public footpaths across farmland**

■ **Use gates and stiles to cross fences, hedges and walls**

■ **Leave livestock, crops and machinery alone**

■ **Take your litter home**

■ **Help to keep all water clean**

■ **Protect wildlife, plants and trees**

■ **Take special care on country roads**

■ **Make no unnecessary noise**

ABOVE RIGHT *Carelessness with cigarettes, matches or camp fires can be devastating in a forest.*

36 QueenAnne's Gate, London SW1H 9AS
Tel: 0171-222 9251.

Most regions of great scenic beauty in England and Wales are designated National Parks or Areas of Outstanding Natural Beauty (AONB). In Scotland, they are known as National Scenic Areas (NSAs) or AONBs.

Most of this land is privately owned and there is no right of public access. In some cases, local authorities may have negotiated agreements with landowners to allow walkers access on mountains and moors.

CONSERVATION
National park, AONB or NSA status is intended to provide some measure of protection for the land-scape, guarding against unsuitable development while encouraging enjoyment of its natural beauty.

Nature reserves are areas set aside for conservation. Most are privately owned, some by large organizations such as the Royal Society for the Protection of Birds. Although some offer public access, most require permission to enter.

THE RAMBLERS ASSOCIATION
The aims of the Ramblers Association are to further greater understanding and care of the countryside, to protect and enhance public rights of way and areas of natural beauty, to improve public access to the countryside, and to encourage more people to take up rambling as a healthy, recreational activity. It has played an important role in preserving and developing our national footpath network.

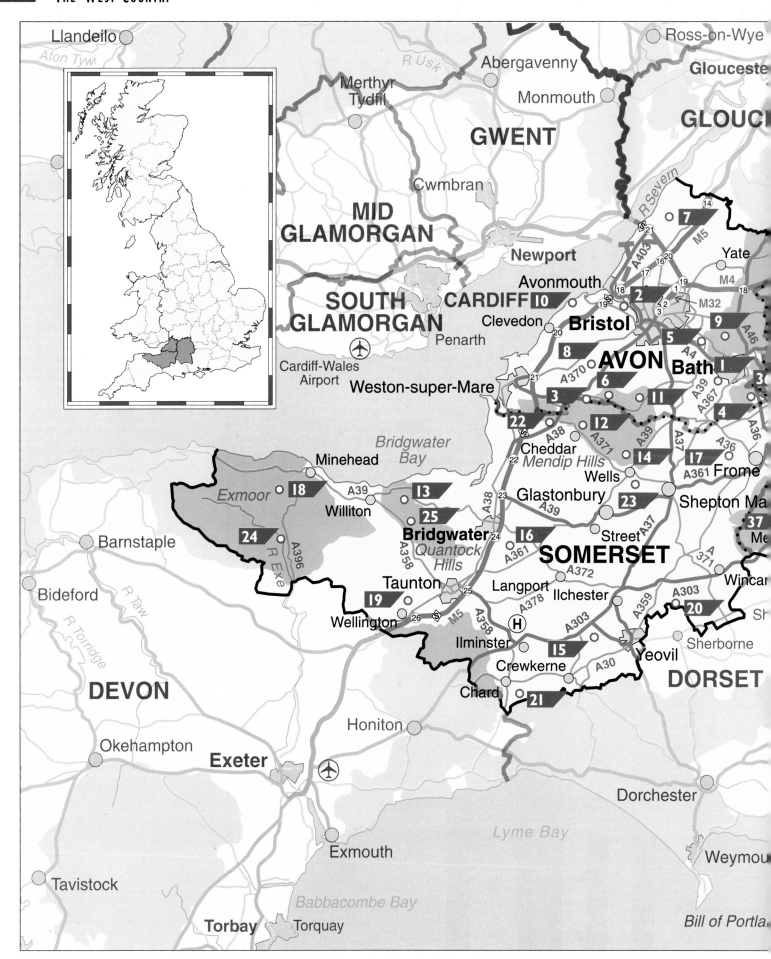

Llandeilo

Afon Tywi

R Usk

Ross-on-Wye

Abergavenny

Merthyr Tydfil

Monmouth

Glouceste

GWENT

Cwmbran

GLOUCI

MID GLAMORGAN

Newport

Yate

Avonmouth

14

7

M5

A403

CARDIFF 10

SOUTH GLAMORGAN

Clevedon

Penarth

Cardiff-Wales Airport

Weston-super-Mare

Bristol

AVON Bath

16 20

17

18

2

19

1

M4

M32

2

3

8

A370

6

5

A4

9

A46

3

A367

11

Bath 1

4

30

22

A38

12

A371

A39

36

A36

Cheddar

22

Mendip Hills

14

17

Frome

Wells

A361

4

36

Minehead

Bridgwater Bay

18

Exmoor

A39

13

Williton

25

Glastonbury

A39

23

Shepton Ma

37

Me

Barnstaple

24

R Exe

A396

A358

Bridgwater

16

Street

A37

SOMERSET

A372

Wincar

Bideford

R Taw

R Torridge

Quantock Hills

24

A361

A303

A359

A303

20

Sh

Taunton

19

25

M5

Langport

A378

Ilchester

Sherborne

Yeovil

DORSET

Wellington

26

A3358

15

H

A303

A30

DEVON

Ilminster

Crewkerne

Okehampton

Chard

21

Exeter

Honiton

Dorchester

Tavistock

Lyme Bay

Exmouth

Weymou

Babbacombe Bay

Torbay Torquay

Bill of Portla

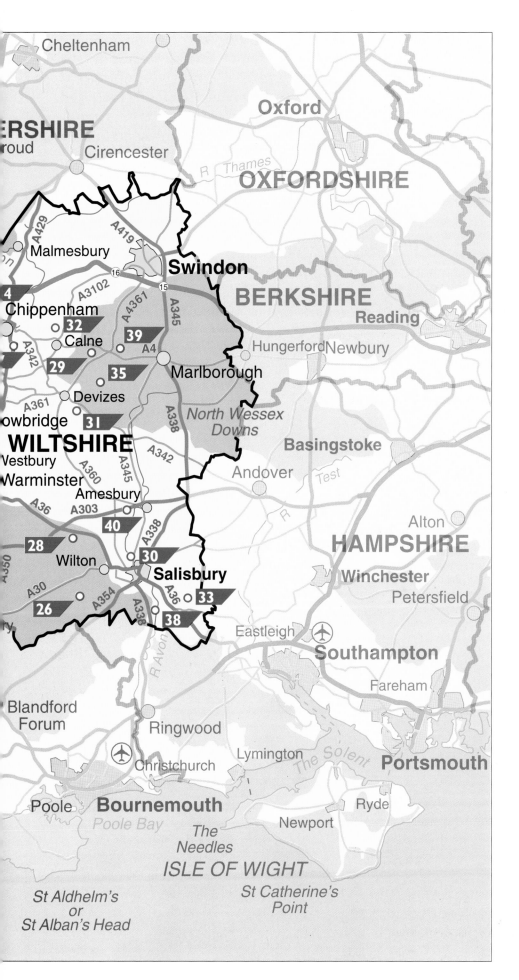

The West Country

All the walks featured in this book are plotted and numbered on the regional map (left) and listed in the box below.

USING MAPS

Although the OUT & ABOUT WALKING GUIDES TO BRITAIN give you all the information you need, it is useful to have some basic map skills. Most of us have some experience of using a motoring atlas to navigate by car. Navigating when walking is much the same, except that mistakes are much more time and energy consuming and, if circumstances conspire, could lead to an accident.

A large-scale map is the answer to identifying where you are. Britain is fortunate in having the best mapping agency in the world, the Ordnance Survey, which produces high-quality maps, the most popular being the 1:50,000 Landranger series. However, the most useful for walkers are the 1:25,000 Pathfinder, Explorer and Outdoor Leisure maps.

THE LIE OF THE LAND

A map provides more than just a bird's eye view of the land; it also conveys information about the terrain – whether marshy, forested, covered with tussocky grass or boulders; it distinguishes between footpaths and bridleways; and shows boundaries such as parish and county boundaries.

Symbols are used to identify a variety of landmarks such as churches, camp and caravan sites, bus, coach and rail stations, castles, caves and historic houses. Perhaps most importantly of all, the shape of the land is indicated by contour lines. Each line represents land at a specific height so it is possible to read the gradient from the spacing of the lines (the closer the spacing, the steeper the hill).

GRID REFERENCES

All Ordnance Survey maps are overprinted with a framework of squares known as the National Grid. This is a reference system which, by breaking the country down into squares, allows you to pinpoint any place in the country and give it a unique reference number; very useful when making rendezvous arrangements. On OS Landranger, Pathfinder and Outdoor Leisure maps it is possible to give a reference to an accuarcy of 100 metres. Grid squares on these maps cover an area of 1 km x 1 km on the ground.

GIVING A GRID REFERENCE

Blenheim Palace in Oxfordshire has a grid reference of **SP 441 161**. This is constructed as follows:

SP These letters identify the 100 km grid square in which Blenheim Palace lies. These squares form the basis of the National Grid. Information on the

100 km square covering a particular map is always given in the map key.

441 161 This six figure reference locates the position of Blenheim Palace to 100 metres in the 100 km grid square.

44 This part of the reference is the number of the grid line which forms the western (left-hand) boundary of the 1 km grid square in which Blenheim Palace appears. This number is printed in the top and bottom margins of the relevant OS map (Pathfinder 1092 in this case).

16 This part of the reference is the number of the grid line which forms the southern (lower) boundary of the 1 km grid square in which Blenheim Palace appears. This number is printed in the left- and right-hand margins of the relevant OS map (Pathfinder 1092).

These two numbers together (SP 4416) locate the bottom left-hand corner of

the 1 km grid square in which Blenheim Palace appears. The remaining figures in the reference **441 161** pinpoint the position within that square by dividing its western boundary lines into tenths and estimating on which imaginary tenths line Blenheim Palace lies.

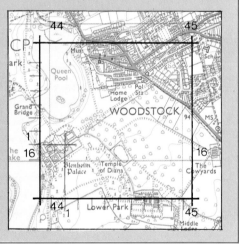

PRISTON MILL

FACT FILE

☀ Englishcombe, near Bath, Avon

🚌 Pathfinder 1183 (ST 66/76), grid reference ST 716628

miles 0 1 2 3 4 5 6 7 8 9 10 miles
kms 0 1 2 3 4 5 6 7 8 9 10 11 12 13 14 15 kms

◔ Allow 2 hours

▭ Gentle walking; there is one short section which is usually wet and muddy

P There are parking spaces in and around the village

🍴 Café and toilets at Priston Mill, Tel. (01225) 460234 for times

◄ *Priston Mill was mainly used to grind corn for cattle feed. (inset) The electric blue flash of a kingfisher by the mill leat is all that is usually seen of this shy bird.*

To an 18th-century working water mill

This gentle stroll through undulating countryside begins at the village of Englishcombe. From the lane outside the church, look out to the right and you can see a pronounced dip in the field, which seems to lead away to the farmhouse on the hill. This is, in fact, part of the Wansdyke Ⓐ, an earthwork of ditch and bank, which once stretched from a point south of Bristol all the way to the Savernake Forest. It is generally thought to have been built by the British leader Ambrosius at the end of the 6th century AD, as a protection against the invading Saxons.

BRIDGE OVER A STREAM

From Englishcombe, the broad track runs between hedgerows crowded with wild flowers in summer. When it narrows down to a footpath between the trees, the path becomes a little wet and muddy, with water running down the gulley. This section ends when the stream is reached with its simple wooden bridge constructed out of old railway sleepers.

Beyond Inglesbatch, the path opens out again with fine views of the undulating Somerset countryside and across to the tower of Priston church. This is a most attractive part of the walk which takes you down to the valley of the busy Conygre Brook, and Priston Mill Ⓑ. There was a mill recorded on this site in the *Domesday Book*, though the present building is not nearly that old.

WATER MILL AT WORK

Priston is a handsome stone mill, built in the 18th century and modernised over a century ago, when the 21 feet (6.3 metres) diameter waterwheel was installed. Water is led down an artificial channel or leat to run into a trough or launder and from here it falls on to the top of the wheel, when the weight of the falling water drives it round. Technically, this is known as a pitchback wheel and supplies the power for all the mill machinery. The grindstones still turn to produce wholemeal flour, and it is a delight to see the simple efficiency of this old machinery at work today.

The area along the leat was once an elm wood, and has now been replanted as a little nature reserve. Here visitors can see a variety of wildfowl from the familiar mallard to the more exotic greylag geese from Iceland, or a buzzard slowly

Wansdyke, an earthwork built in the 6th century to keep out the Saxons.

THE WALK

ENGLISHCOMBE — PRISTON

Park in the village of Englishcombe. The walk starts at the church from where there is a view of Wansdyke Ⓐ.

1 Go down the steps from the churchyard and turn left into the lane. At Manor Farm turn right on to the road marked 'No Through Road'. The road soon ends, but is continued as a rough, stony track.

2 The broad track veers left towards a field. The route now continues straight on down a narrow footpath, completely overhung by trees like a green tunnel. The path continues downhill to a footbridge over the stream, then climbs up the hill again.

3 At the roadway turn right and right again by the telephone box down the road waymarked as a dead end.

4 At Virginia House turn right down the track signposted 'Mill Lane'. Follow the path through the gate and then, after a short length of track, through a second gate into a field. Cross the field, go over a stile, then pass through the gap in the hedge, keeping the line of trees at the field boundary to your left. Cross the stream by the footbridge and follow the path to the mill Ⓑ and farm up ahead.

5 Beyond the mill, turn right through the visitors' car park and then when the concrete path veers off to the right, continue straight on along the broad grassy track to the farm gate. Follow the track uphill to another gate into a field. The next stile is met by taking a line between the prominent clump of trees on the brow of the hill and the row of telegraph poles. Turn slightly to the right and head towards the tall oak tree in a clump of trees. Cross the footbridge and take the path through the field to the village of Wilmington.

6 Cross the stile, and at the road turn right. Follow the tarmac road, ignoring the rough track turning downhill at the right opposite Pennsylvania Farm Ⓒ.

7 At the foot of the hill, the road swings sharply round to the left. At this point continue straight on, leaving the road for the footpath. Cross the bridge over the stream, climb over the stile on the right and take the path through the cornfield. Cross the stile at the end of the field, take the path round the pond and go left of the three-storey stone house for the gate opposite the steps to the churchyard where the walk started.

circling, high above the hill.

The walk over the hill to Wilmington provides wide vistas over gently rolling farmland. The road is a quiet country lane with more splendid views across the countryside. By Pennsylvania Farm Ⓒ, with its pretty stone farmhouse, there is a second chance to view the ancient Wansdyke earthworks.

There is one other old site on view in the last part of the walk. As you approach the church at Englishcombe, you can see a large artificial mound which is all that remains of a medieval castle.

▲ *The footpath goes through a cornfield on the way back to Englishcombe.*
▶ *Conygre Brook is a swift-running stream which feeds the mill.*

THE AVON GORGE

Through lush woodland on the edge of a dramatic gorge

This is a walk through the National Nature Reserve, Leigh Woods, and along the bank of the Avon in the spectacular limestone gorge. It plunges straight into the broad-leaved woodland where oak is the dominant species, but where ash, elm, birch, lime, beech and sycamore are also found. The woodland is so all-enveloping that it is difficult to believe that the city of Bristol is nearby.

A short walk leads to a clearing and the warden's cottage, but beyond these lie the massive ramparts of Stokeleigh Camp **Ⓐ**. This is an Iron Age fort, built late in the third century BC and occupied for about 200 years. (This may have been a troubled period in British history, for such heavily fortified camps can be found through the country.)

FORTIFICATIONS

The steep bank of the Avon gorge provides ample protection against attack on one side, and the landward side is protected by a horseshoe of ditches and ramparts. There are actually three lines of ramparts, but it is the innermost one that is the most impressive, rising to a height of 29 1/2 feet (9 metres).

The path cuts through the middle of the fort and turns towards the rim of the gorge to arrive at a splendid viewpoint **Ⓑ** above the River Avon. To the right is the famous suspension bridge, designed by Isambard Kingdom Brunel. In 1829, a competition was organised for a bridge over the Avon and Brunel, then only

The Bristol whitebeam is found nowhere else in the world but the Avon Gorge.

▲ *Clifton suspension bridge over Avon Gorge. The green hellebore (inset) is a woodland plant that blooms in February.*

23 years old, was the winner. Work began in 1831, but funds ran out and it was not completed until 1864, after Brunel's death.

The opposite bank of the river is notable for the great range of limestone cliffs, above which can be seen the little round tower of the camera obscura. Here you stand in a dark room and watch a moving image of

FACT FILE

- ⚹ Leigh Woods, near Bristol, Avon

- 🚗 Pathfinder 1166 (ST 47/57), grid reference ST 555730

  miles 0 1 2 3 4 5 6 7 8 9 10 miles
  kms 0 1 2 3 4 5 6 7 8 9 10 11 12 13 14 15 kms

- 🕐 Allow 1 3/4 hours

- ▬ Easy walking, but steep descent to river, which is slippery after rain

- P North Road by stile and notice board for Avon Gorge National Nature Reserve

- 🍴 For cafés, pubs, shops and toilets, cross the suspension bridge to Clifton (there is a small toll)
- WC

THE WALK

LEIGH WOODS

To reach the start of the walk, cross the Clifton suspension bridge from Bristol and turn right into North Road. Park near the stile leading into Leigh Woods by the notice board for the Avon Gorge National Nature Reserve.

1 Cross the stile and enter the woodland. The path immediately divides: take the path to the left, going slightly uphill.

2 At the small green with cottages on the left, take the path bearing off to the right. The path leads to the Iron Age fortress, Stokeleigh Camp **A**.

3 At the fence by the rim of the gorge **B**, turn left.

4 At the ditch on the far side of the fort, where the path divides by the pond, take the path to the right, and immediately beyond that turn right again.

5 By the stone wall, where the path divides,

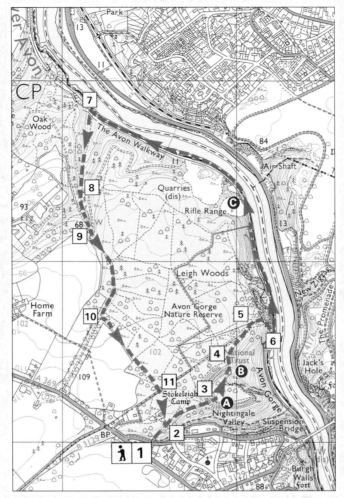

take the narrow path to the right going steeply downhill.

6 At the gravel track by the riverside turn left. You are now walking on the Avon Walkway **C**.

7 Where the path divides, turn left under the high arched railway bridge, back into the woodland.

8 Where the path divides, continue straight up on the path to the left.

9 At the next junction, turn right on to the trackway to Oakwood Lodge. Turn left by the lodge and continue on the broad gravel track.

10 At the edge of the woodland turn left on to the path, keeping in the wood with the field to the right.

11 Continue straight on through the gap in the wall and carry on to the small green with cottages at stage **2**. Retrace your steps to the start.

◀ *This long flat slab is typical of the rocks found in the gorge.*
▶ *The wildness of Leigh Woods is protected by its status as a nature reserve.*

the world outside. The path continues around the rim of the gorge, where the woods thin out slightly and there are more views of the buildings of Clifton across the river.

The path leaves the fort through a gap in the ramparts by a small pond. The route then goes downhill on a narrow path, which is very steep in places, leading to the riverside path, the Avon Walkway **C**. This runs alongside the Avon for 27 1/2 miles (44 km), from Pill near the Bristol Channel to the Dundas Aqueduct on

the Kennet and Avon Canal. Looking back one can see the warehouses clustered around the entrance to Bristol Docks.

An arch to the left of the walk carries the railway line to Portishead, now virtually disused. Those who wonder how they crossed the line without noticing it can be assured it was not an oversight: the path goes over the top of a short tunnel.

PATH THROUGH THE WOOD

The path turns up into the woods, where the railway crosses the deep valley on a high arched bridge. This is an altogether denser section of woodland, with a mixture of broad-leaved trees and conifers. There is a good deal of wildlife: birds and

squirrels are common, and badger setts can be seen. At Oakwood Lodge, the path takes to the broad driveway before turning back to run close to the fields of a local farm for the return to the start.

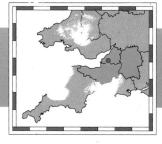

Over Dolebury Hill to an Iron Age hillfort

Burrington Combe is a smaller version of the famous Cheddar Gorge, formed by an ancient river which, thousands of years ago, found a new, underground route. The massive rock **A** with the deep cleft down the middle provided shelter in the 18th century for the Reverend A M Toplady and was the inspiration for his famous hymn:

Rock of Ages, cleft for me
Let me hide myself in thee.

◀ *The original Rock of Ages, after which the famous hymn was named.*

The cave on the hillside beyond the rock, Aveline's Hole, was occupied at the end of the Ice Age, about 900 years ago.

Climbing the hill, you emerge from the woodland to a broad expanse of bracken-covered moor. A large dip to the left of the track **B** leads to the entrance to Rod's Pot. This is one of a whole series of caves with which the Mendip Hills, a popular area for potholers, are riddled. This is an area of rough moorland, liberally sprinkled with hawthorn.

HILLTOP GRASSLANDS

At the crown of the hill, the bracken gives way to the grassland of Dolebury Warren, an area now in the care of the National Trust. Rabbit warrens were once an important part of the rural economy. They were, however, generally the preserves of the lord of the manor and the rabbits were valued both for their pelts and for their meat.

As you walk the close-cropped grassland, there are magnificent views out over the Mendips and the surrounding countryside. On the

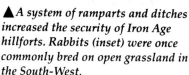

▲ *A system of ramparts and ditches increased the security of Iron Age hillforts. Rabbits (inset) were once commonly bred on open grassland in the South-West.*

FACT FILE

☀ Burrington Combe, Avon

▭ Pathfinder 1198 (ST 45/55), grid reference ST 476587

miles 0 1 2 3 4 5 6 7 8 9 10 miles
kms 0 1 2 3 4 5 6 7 8 9 10 11 12 13 14 15 kms

◐ 2¹/₂ hours

▬ Steep and muddy in places, so good walking shoes are recommended

P On the B3134 at Rock of Ages

▦ Light snacks and drinks available throughout the day at Burrington Inn pub.

WC Toilets at adjacent car park

THE WALK

DOLEBURY WARREN

The walk starts in the public car park in Burrington Combe next to the Burrington Inn, opposite the Rock of Ages A on the B3134.

1 From the car park turn right along the road past the Burrington Inn. At the nursery gardens, cross the road and take the footpath uphill to the left of The Cottage. When you reach the roadway, turn left and continue on in this direction after the road turns into a broad track.

2 Where the path divides by a wooden gate, continue straight on. Beyond the house, the broad track swings to the right, and is marked 'Private'. Continue straight on past the entrance to the Rod's Pot caves B. Where the path divides with the conifer plantation ahead on the left, take the path that leads around to the right.

3 Where the path divides by the woodland (with the plantation to the left), turn right by the field wall. Then, after 50 yards (45 metres), turn left and cross the stile on to Dolebury Warren. Ignoring the path to the right, continue straight on through the patch of scrub woodland. The route then continues on through the middle of the hillfort C.

4 Leave the hillfort by the gap in the ramparts and take the broad path which swings at first around to the left, then back around to the right. Just before a house, the path divides. Turn right to cross the stile. Continue along the path through the woods and scrubland and cross the stile over the fence on the right.

5 Where the path divides in the clearing, turn left downhill towards the conifers. Cross the stile and follow the steep, winding path.

6 At the fields, turn right and follow the path through the conifers. At the end go through a gate to the houses. Turn left, cross the stile ahead and turn right to follow the track that bears left in front of a building. Follow this track, gradually climbing up the hill. Where the path divides, take the path that leads around to the right.

7 At the clearing, do not cross the stile, but continue along the path to the left that follows the field edge.

8 At the broad track turn left, going downhill. Opposite the gate with the stile on the left, take the path to the right through the woodland. Almost immediately after this the track divides. Take the route to the left that curves around the hill past a ruined building.

9 When you reach the roadway, turn left, then right on to the footpath to retrace your steps back to Burrington Combe and the car park at the start of the walk.

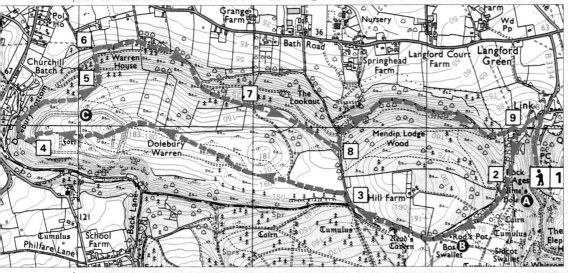

horizon, the most obvious features are the high banks that mark the presence of Dolebury hillfort C. This hillfort was constructed in the Iron Age, a period which lasted from around 500 BC until the time of the Roman occupation.

The Celtic tribes of Britain used such hilltop sites for defensive purposes, supplementing the natural advantages of steep slopes by enclosing the settlement with massive ramparts and deep ditches. Not all the bumps and hollows that can be seen on this site are the marks left by these Iron Age settlers, however; in later years, there was a good deal of lead mining in the hills.

▶ *The final stretch of the walk goes through woodland, rich in wildlife.*

The gap at the far end of the ramparts marks the original west gate, which, because the approach is so steep, has less elaborate defences than that at the east. On the northern side of the hill, the open moorland gives way to often dense woodland, a mixture of broad-leaved trees and conifers, where wood pigeon, pheasant and squirrels can frequently be seen. The path rises and falls, following a switch-back course along the side of the hill before coming out on the path back to Burrington Combe.

AVON

This was the chapter house where priory meetings were held, and there was a library on the top floor. There are also remains of the refectory and excavation has shown that there was originally a cloister, 226 ft square (4,600 sq metres), around which were grouped 14 small houses or cells.

OLD GATEHOUSE

During Henry VIII's dissolution of the monasteries the old gatehouse was incorporated into a new dwelling. The splendid house that you can see received its last major alterations late in the 16th century.

The walk continues across grassy fields to the small settlement of

FACT FILE

✳ Hinton Charterhouse, Avon

▭ Pathfinder 1199 (ST 65/75), grid reference ST 776583

miles 0 1 2 3 4 5 6 7 8 9 10 miles
kms 0 1 2 3 4 5 6 7 8 9 10 11 12 13 14 15 kms

◔ Allow 4 hours

◼ Steep in places and muddy in patches, but generally good walking

🅿 In the lane off the minor road by Hinton Charterhouse Church

🍴 At Hinton Charterhouse, Midford and Combe Hay

Explore an unusual system of disused railways and canals

▲*Cam Brook is a spawning ground for the hairy dragonfly (inset). The viaduct of the local Limpley Stoke line threads through the arches of the Somerset and Dorset railway (right).*

Despite the industrial nature of this walk, it begins by passing a magnificent stately home and a medieval priory.

Hinton House was built in 1701. It presents a handsomely classical frontage to the world, with pedimented windows and a porch with Ionic columns, the whole effect completed by the balustrade that runs above the walls. The park is grassland, dotted with mature trees.

Across the road are the remains of Hinton Priory ❹. This was the Charter House that gave the village its name. Founded in 1232, the same year as Lacock Abbey, it is one of the oldest Carthusian houses in England. The main building is a tower with a gabled roof and is built in a simple style with buttresses and lancet windows.

THE WALK

HINTON CHARTERHOUSE – COMBE HAY

The walk beings at Hinton Charterhouse Church.

1 Enter the iron gate and walk through the churchyard in the direction indicated by the sign 'Public Footpath'. Leave by the gate in the churchyard wall and cross the parkland in the direction indicated by the arrow. Aim for the prominent group of conifers. Cross the stile at the roadway and continue straight across to the stile opposite by the footpath sign, then head for the stile opposite the priory **A**.

2 Beyond the priory, cross the stile, turn right for the next stile and continue straight on. There is now a series of stiles crossing the field fences. At the houses, continue across the broad track to take the path between the houses. At the roadway turn left past the thatched cottage. Do not cross the stile but continue on the broad track.

3 Where the concrete farm path turns right — at the top of the hill where you get a good view over Midford Castle **B** — continue straight on down the narrow lane. This lane gets narrower and steeper as you go along. At the end of the path, cross the road and go over the footbridge by the mill and follow the causeway across the field. When you reach the roadway, turn right.

4 At the main road turn right under the viaduct **C**, then immediately right onto the public footpath opposite the Hope and Anchor. Just beyond the old canal bridge, cross the stile and turn left to take the path under the railway bridge, then rejoin the walk by the canal towpath. Walk past a ruined stone bridge, the Radstock aqueduct **D**. Continue along the towpath.

5 At the buildings at the end of the wide grassy track, cross over the road, go under the railway bridge and continue to follow the line of the old canal, past the locks. At the top of the locks — where the canal

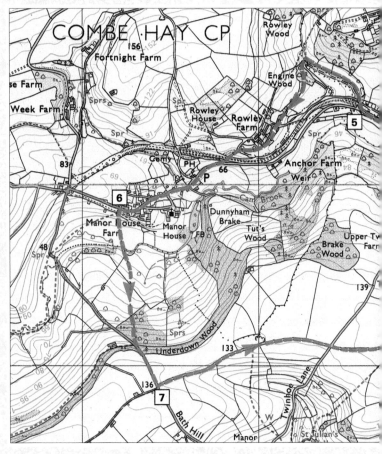

does a U-turn — do not cross the stile, but take the path round to the left going up through the woods. At the top of the woods, cross the canal as indicated by footpath sign and cross the field to the next stile. Then turn left as at the sign. At the road junction beyond Rowley Farm, turn right and follow that road.

6 Continue past the church, then turn left to

Pipehouse. After that you join a track that begins as a broad avenue flanked by oak trees, but gradually closes in until it becomes a very steep gully running between high banks. The building to the right, looking like an overgrown Olympic torch, is a water tower. At the higher point of the hill there are views over to the right of the 18th-century house, Midford Castle **B**, while down in the valley on the left is a curious building with a pyramidal roof. This is a malting house. The roof covers the kiln where barley is

◀*An overgrown bridge carries an old cart track across the disused Somerset Coal Canal, proving even old industrial architecture can be picturesque.*

cross the stile in the stone wall. Continue across the fields, leaving the obelisk on your left. At the roadway, turn left.

7 At the road junction turn left, towards Twinhoe. At the crossroads, continue straight on. Where the road divides at Middle Twinhoe, turn right then, when the road swings left, turn right onto the concreted track. Go through the gate marked with a yellow arrow and continue following the path around the edges of the fields. The path becomes a green lane leading down to Wellow Brook.

8 At the house, turn right down the hill under the disused railway, keeping to the right and continue onto the brook. Cross the brook by the footbridge and follow the path uphill to the right through the coppiced wood **E**. Continue upstream through the valley to the lane.

9 At the crossroads, turn right past the Stag Inn. Turn left at the Rose and Crown pub to return to the start of the walk.

heated. At the end of the path is the village of Midford, with an old water mill beside the stream. The scene up ahead is dominated by what looks like one big railway viaduct **C**.

TWO VIADUCTS

When you reach it, you discover there is not one viaduct but two, the second threading its way under the arches of the first. The road itself crosses the brook on an old stone bridge. After the Hope and Anchor pub up on the main road a footpath now runs down to the towpath of the derelict Somerset Coal Canal.

The canal runs along the bottom of the valley, mimicking the winding path of the Cam Brook. This is a particularly attractive section of the walk, with green fields on the valley floor, and oak woodland rising up the bank beyond the canal. On the left you can see what appears to be a ruined stone bridge **D** over the brook. This is an aqueduct that carried a branch of the canal down to Radstock. As you climb up the valley, the canal begins to climb through a series of locks, at first well spaced, then coming closer together. The canal swings away through woodland dominated by massive beech trees, then suddenly does a complete U-turn in Engine Wood to head up towards Combe Hay. The footpath takes a more direct route so it comes as a surprise after climbing the hill to find your-

▲*In some places the old Somerset Coal Canal has been partially filled in and has become overgrown. Gradually it is returning to the wild.*

▼Combe Hay's Georgian Manor is surrounded by well-trimmed lawns that slope down to a rotunda and an ornamental lake. The pub in Combe Hay has its own dovecot (right).

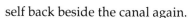

self back beside the canal again.

Combe Hay is an attractive village of mellow stone houses. Old Rectory enjoys a fine position with wide views over the surrounding, rolling countryside. Beyond the church you leave the road for a path past the 18th-century Combe Hay Manor. In the grounds you can see an obelisk and, in the distance, a little rotunda beside an ornamental lake. The path climbs up the hill on the opposite side of Cam Brook, with yet more splendid views out over a wide stretch of country all the way to the outskirts of Bath.

The footpath gives way to roadway, but this is a quiet country lane running between high hedges. The views are still magnificent and you can see other similar lanes, bordered by hedges looking from a distance like long furry caterpillars.

MEANDERING STREAM

The road gives way again to a footpath at the hamlet of Twinhoe. The way drops down to yet another peaceful valley with a gently meandering stream. Beyond the stream is an area of coppiced woodland **Ⓔ**. These are managed woods in which shoots from the stump are grown up as 'poles', which are then harvested and a new set of shoots begins to grow again.

A tiny tributary stream has cut a deep cleft in the hillside up which the path climbs to Hinton Charterhouse. The village is notable for its old stone houses and makes a fitting finale to the walk.

▼Hinton Priory is the second-oldest Carthusian house in England, after Witham Friary.

The Somerset Coal Canal

It seems strange to think of this area of Avon having any connection with industry. But in fact it lies at the edge of the extensive Somerset coalfield, which was worked until the 1970s.

In 1805, the Somerset Coal Canal was opened, linking the mining area to the Kennet and Avon Canal at Limpley Stoke. There were two branches: the main canal which the walk follows and the southerly route from Radstock. All that remains of the latter is the ruined aqueduct over the Cam Brook.

The main branch swings north and climbs up the hill to Combe Hay, via 22 locks and the great about-turn

at Engine Wood. Originally it continued on towards the foot of Combe Hill, up which the boats were transported by a 'caisson lock'. This was a giant waterproof iron cylinder that boats could be floated into. The cylinder was immersed in a water-filled pit. Once the boat was inside, the door was shut behind it. Air was pumped into the cylinder, forcing water out and making the cylinder light enough to float to the top of the pit. There the cylinder was opened and the boat floated off. All traces of this device have now disappeared, apart from the name which lives on in Caisson House.

The canal was closed in 1889 when the railway to Limpley Stoke took over. For part of the way the line was built over the old canal — it made use of the canal tunnel beyond Combe Hay. The regular train service ended in 1951, but in 1953 the line was used in the film *The Titfield Thunderbolt*. A feature of this line was the viaduct that passed under the arches of the Somerset and Dorset railway.

In the 19th century, a comprehensive system of canals carried goods the length and breadth of England.

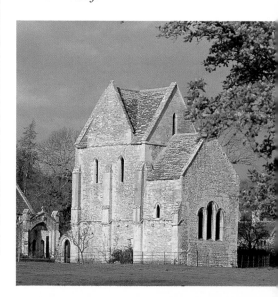

AVON

brought a vast amount of new boating activity to the river, as can be seen from the bustling marina by the bridge. The waterway was not, however, built with pleasure boating in mind. Two centuries ago, Keynsham was the centre of a thriving brass industry. Avon mill, upstream from the bridge and dignified by a little cupola, was once used for brass-working. The mill featured no fewer than eight water wheels to run the appropriate machinery.

◀ *A late-afternoon view along the Avon just west of Bath — once a busy waterway, it is now devoted to leisure uses. Each spike of the tufted vetch (below) can carry up to 30 flowers.*

A walk along a towpath and an embankment that ends in Bath

This walk follows the towpath of the Avon navigation and the disused railway between Bitton and Bath, with a visit to a preserved railway. The return can be made on one of the regular trains that run from Bath to Keynsham.

Since the walk is linear it can be followed in the reverse direction. Those arriving by car will, however, find it much easier to park in Keynsham than in Bath.

ACROSS THE AVON

From Keynsham the walk begins with a short stroll down the road to the bridge across the Avon. At this point the river divides: to one side the water thunders over a weir, while to the other it passes down an artificial cutting Ⓐ in which a lock allows boats to pass easily up and

▶ *Water pours through a pair of lock gates on the River Avon as they open to allow a boat to proceed upstream.*

down. The building of the locks to make the Avon navigable between Bristol and Bath was completed in 1723. Now, however, the Avon navigation is part of an even longer waterway system, joined by the Kennet and Avon Canal to the River Thames at Reading.

Some years ago, most of the canal was derelict, but in 1990 it was reopened throughout. This has

FACT FILE

✳ Keynsham

🖭 Pathfinder 1183 (ST66/76), grid reference ST 656689

miles 0 1 2 3 4 5 6 7 8 9 10 miles
kms 0 1 2 3 4 5 6 7 8 9 10 11 12 13 14 15 kms

🕐 Allow 4 hours

▭ Easy going on good paths

🅿 Station car park at Keynsham. If this is full there is a car park beside the first bridge on the route

🏛🍴 Full range of facilities at Keynsham and Bath. Pub beside the walk at Saltford

THE WALK

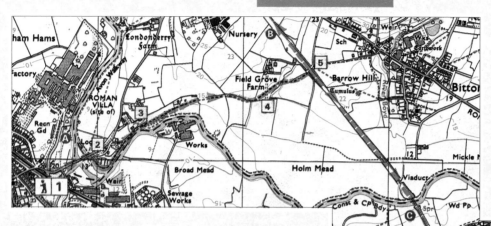

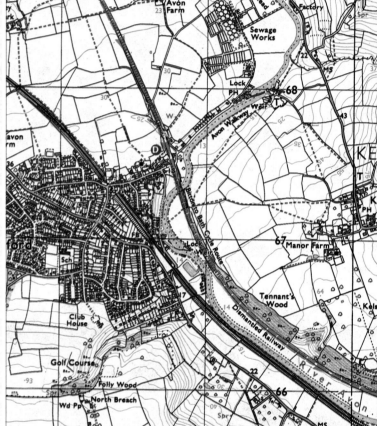

KEYNSHAM – CENTRAL BATH

The walk begins at Keynsham station and ends at Bath station.

1 From Keynsham station turn right to follow the main road downhill.

2 Cross the main stream of the river and the lock cutting **Ⓐ**. Turn right by the car park and follow the signs marked 'Avon Walkway' down to the river bank. Follow the towpath beside the river, signposted to Swineford.

3 Where the towpath meets the broad track, turn left and follow the latter towards the large, square house. At the house, leave the broad track for the footpath, which continues straight on, following the line of the telegraph poles. It continues across the fields via a series of stiles.

4 Cross the stile on the left by the farm buildings and continue in the direction indicated by the yellow arrow here. At the broad track leading up to the farm, turn diagonally to the right, past a stone barn. Continue on the path via more stiles, heading towards the prominent railway bridge.

5 At the bridge, take the path up the right-hand side of the arch to reach the top of the embankment. Turn left to visit the steam railway **Ⓑ**, about 1,100 yards (1 km) along the embankment. Then return to this point and continue towards Bath. The route continues straight on along the old railway, over the first of the river viaducts **Ⓒ** and past the village of Saltford **Ⓓ**.

6 Immediately beyond the bridge across the river on the outskirts of Bath, turn right past the drinking fountain to the towpath. Continue in the same direction along the towpath to the heart of the city **Ⓔ**.

7 The towpath ends at Broad Quay. Continue straight on down Dorchester Street to the station for trains back to Keynsham.

A more likely-looking candidate for heavy industry can be seen downstream, where the view is dominated by a bulky red-brick factory with a tall chimney. It is not, however, brass they make here, but chocolate. The factory, is in fact, part of the Cadbury empire.

The walk briefly follows the towpath of the River Avon — a

◀The church tower in Bitton village, which can be seen from the vantage-point of the railway embankment.

reminder that in the early working days of the navigation, boats were pulled by horses. Soon, however, the path strikes off across the fields. To the right, across the river, you can see the present main railway line from Bristol to Bath, while up ahead is the high embankment of the disused railway, the next stage of the walk. A high-arched bridge carries the former line, and it is here that walkers join the railway route.

After the line's closure in 1971, a local organization was set up with the aim of converting the track-bed into a safe inter-city route for cyclists and walkers. The scheme has proved a great success — there are similar schemes in other areas.

But there are still trains to be seen at the old Bitton station. By turning left on the embankment, you come to the track **ⓑ**, where steam and diesel locomotives are to be seen at work on open days.

THE HIGH GROUND

Returning to the bridge and continuing towards Bath, you soon discover one of the advantages of walking old railways: the embankment provides an airy viewpoint for seeing the surrounding countryside. To the right, you look across the flat fields to the river, while to the left is the village of Bitton, with its prominent church tower and the hills rising behind it. Between the bank and the village is a rounded, grassy hump, a prehistoric burial site or round barrow, still remembered by the name Barrow Hill.

The approach to the river is marked by lines of pollarded willows along the hedgerows. Once across the first of the river viaducts **ⓒ** a picnic area offers the first sight of the 'sculpture trail' laid out along the walkway. Here large blocks of stone have been covered with vari-

▶ *One of the large carvings in the sculpture trail that embellishes one side of the river. The Saxon style of the sculptures alludes to a nearby Anglo-Saxon burial ground.*

ous devices: faces, a jar, a short sword, a shield and so on. The theme is Saxon, reflecting the fact that an Anglo-Saxon burial ground is sited close by.

Gradually the track cuts deeper into the ground, in a familiar pattern of railway building. The engineers dug a cutting through the rising ground, and used the spoil to build up the embankment across the valley. It creates a rather secretive, enclosed world, undisturbed except by the songs of birds.

Now, instead of the line crossing over lanes and roads, it goes beneath them, and one can see the simple, no-nonsense style of the bridges, built with stone abutments and brick arches.

A KISSING SEAT

At Saltford **ⓓ** there is easy access to the village, via steps that go down past the Bird in Hand public house. Continuing across the river, you will encounter a 'kissing seat' — another sculptured feature — with a view over boathouses and the lock. Among the buildings downstream

from the lock you can just make out a stone chimney, marking the remains of another old brass mill.

The nature of the walk changes again, now running along the side of a hill. To the right is the river, and alongside is the railway line, which

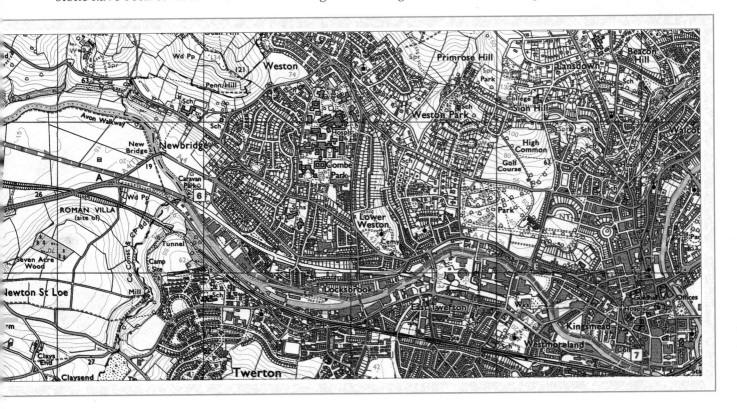

once belonged to the Great Western Railway. To the left, the hill is wooded with coppice trees, interspersed with solitary tall oaks and rows of young birch along the track. By the next bridge is another carved seat, ingeniously created from interlocking former railway sleepers.

BATH STONE

The road soon crosses the track, and it is worth looking at the underside of the 19th-century bridge to see the construction technique, with brick arches between the girders supporting the roadway. Beyond the bridge, you can look across to your left to see the 18th-century road bridge over the river. It provides the first hint of the architectural elegance for which Bath is famous. The whole structure is built from the beautiful, richly coloured Bath stone.

The next bridge marks the end of the railway section of this walk. To the right across the bridge is the last of the sculptures, a fountain that

▼ *The final part of the walk encounters this handsome bridge, its style reminiscent of the elegant buildings to be found in the heart of the city.*

A Station from the Age of Steam

Much of this walk is along the line of the former Midland Railway route from Bath to Mangotsfield on the outskirts of Bristol, where the track once joined the main line from Gloucester to Bristol. Bitton has the last surviving station along the route, a simple, single-storey building, now home to the Avon Valley preserved railway. It has retained a good deal of its old atmosphere: the original Midland Railway lamp standards still look down over the platform, with its old weighing machine, and behind the main station buildings are the former goods warehouses.

There is always a good deal to see here. Carriages still line up beside the platform, two of which belonged to the London, Midland and Scottish (Railway) before nationalization. In the sidings are an old steam crane and trucks and wagons. An old locomotive awaits reconstruction; it is of a type first designed for the Midland Railway and was also in use on the Somerset and Dorset Joint Railway, which once

linked up with this line at Bath.

The railway is seen at its best, however, on those weekends when it goes back to work. Steam locomotives, dating back to 1918, join more recent diesels to give passenger rides along a short length of track. The line has been extended since services were started up again in 1983 and the plan is once again to run trains into Bath.

Lovers of steam railways will find a veritable paradise if they visit Bitton station.

not only supplies drinking water but sends a stream coursing through the carved rock. Beyond it is the river towpath, which you will follow into the heart of the city.

The first part of this towpath walk provides a view of working Bath, rather than the tourist spa. Across the river you can see a battlemented tower — not part of some medieval castle, but the portal of the railway tunnel. Then you come to a lock, with curious metal constructions rising alongside. These, in fact, act as flood barriers.

The river runs through an industrialized area here, and it is interesting to compare the red brick of the older works with the metal and plastic of the new. The railway

once more crosses the river, but it is now no longer part of the cycleway. Beyond it are the gasometers of the former Bath Gas Works, established in 1818.

A little suspension bridge crosses the river. It was designed by a local man, James Dredge, shortly after he had lost the competition for the construction of the Clifton Bridge in Bristol. This marks the first view of one of the splendid Bath terraces, in the centre of the city **E**.

The railway crosses the river for the last time, to the former Green Park station, now converted into a supermarket. Across the water, the river is lined by a timber wharf and a succession of old mills, now converted to offices. On your side, next to the towpath, are fashionable houses, some with ornate balconies, providing a fascinating contrast between the two sides of the river in this final stretch of the walk.

The towpath ends near the heart of the city, and you can now either go on to explore Bath or continue to the station for the return trip by mainline railway to Keynsham.

CIRCLING BLAGDON LAKE

A lakeside walk through woodland and along country lanes

▲*Blagdon Lake is a reservoir 1.65 miles (2.65 km) long. Filling it began in 1899 and top level was reached in 1903. When in bloom, water-lilies (right) open for only a few hours each day.*

A quiet country lane leads from Blagdon village to Blagdon Lake. From the lane there are good views of the lake, its edges dotted with woods and copses, some planted with conifers and ornamental trees. The walk circuits the whole of the lake and includes a visit to the vast Victorian steam engines at the Bristol Waterworks Company.

The walk begins at the village of Blagdon, or rather one part of the village, for it is divided into three distinct sections — East End, West End and Street End. This is the East End, where the two most prominent buildings are the church and the inn. St Andrew's Church Ⓐ with its tall, slender tower, typical of this part of the country, seems ancient but only

FACT FILE

✳ Blagdon, between A38 and A363

🗺 Pathfinders 1198 (ST 45/55) and 1182 (ST 46/56), grid reference ST 504589

miles 0 1 2 3 4 5 6 7 8 9 10 miles
kms 0 1 2 3 4 5 6 7 8 9 10 11 12 13 14 15 kms

◗ Allow 3 hours

▭ The paths become very muddy in wet weather

P Blagdon, near New Inn

T Infrequent bus service from Bristol; Tel. (0117) 9311113 for times

🏛 Full range of facilities at Blagdon

the tower is old. The rest, complete with its gargoyles outside and finely carved rood screen inside, dates only to the beginning of the century.

If the church looks old, but is new, the New Inn paradoxically is genuinely old. It has an interesting sign, with a painting of the inn itself with the sign outside and, on that sign, a picture of the inn — and so

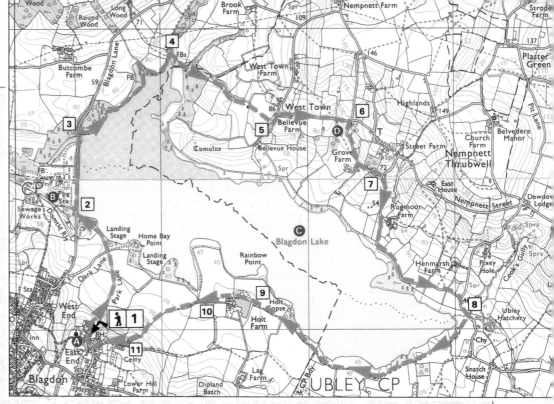

THE WALK

BLAGDON — BLAGDON LAKE

The walk begins at the New Inn at Blagdon, close by the village church Ⓐ.

1 Take the road downhill, past the inn, towards the lake.

2 At the road junction, turn right to follow the road across the dam, past the pumping station Ⓑ below.

3 At the far side of the dam, turn right to cross a stile by the public footpath sign to join the path through the wood. The path soon divides, but keep to the right following the shore, to the far end of the lake Ⓒ.

4 At the end of the lake, cross the stile and turn right over the bridge. Continue straight on over a second stile into the field and keep straight on, close to the wire fence. Cross another stile and a bridge. Keep on the path that continues slightly uphill through the woodland, across another stile, then straight on following the line of the woods, through a gap in the hedge.

5 At the road turn left, then a short distance up the road turn right.

6 At the crossroads turn right to head downhill, past a viewpoint Ⓓ across the lake to Blagdon.

7 At the road junction keep to the right, going downhill.

8 At the junction, turn right, signposted to Ubley and West Harptree. Immediately beyond the small wood, where a fine copper beech overhangs the road, turn right on to the footpath. The path closely follows the Waterworks road along the lakeside.

9 Just before the big modern barns, the footpath crosses two little footbridges to continue on the opposite side of the hedge, then continues past the barns, which you leave to your left. Beyond the barns, cross the stile ahead and go across the field to the left-hand corner.

10 At the broad farm track, turn right. At the first pair of gates take the gate to the left. Follow the track to the second pair of gates and take the left gate to head uphill across the fields. Follow the hedge boundary to a stile ahead to join a deep, overhung lane.

11 At the top of the lane turn right, then right again at the roadway (Church Street) to return to the crossroads by the church and the New Inn.

---

on. The garden at the back of the inn has a magnificent view of the lake, which is the centrepiece of the walk.

Blagdon Lake Ⓒ is not a natural feature, but a reservoir created by damming the River Yeo. The long, straight line of the dam rules off the end of the lake, while to the left is the handsome Inspection House, with verandah, built for the superintendent of the works and having a suitably splendid view across them. As the road comes down to the water's edge, over to the right is a black and white timbered building; this is the fishermen's lodge.

The shallow waters at the edge of the lake are popular with a variety of birds. Apart from the common swans, mallard, coot and moorhen you can often catch sight of a great crested grebe. This attractive bird has an astonishing courtship dance, which is performed in the spring, and a little later in the year the adults can be seen with the young perched on their backs, safe from predatory pike.

TROUT BREEDING

Some very impressive features can be seen from the road that crosses the dam. To the left of the dam, in an area that could well be mistaken for an ornamental park, stand two red Gothic houses with a brick 'tower' in between.

This is Blagdon pumping station Ⓑ, which originally housed four huge steam engines. The tower is the truncated chimney. A century ago, public utilities such as Bristol Waterworks, who were responsible

◄ *Blagdon pumping station is a late Victorian building where four beam engines pumped water until 1949.*

for the creation of the reservoir, were very keen to give such installations an air of grandeur. The engine houses have suitably imposing entrances, with studded wooden doors flanked by stone columns. The house on the left holds two preserved steam engines, while that on the right contains the comparatively small electric pumps that have taken over the work.

The grounds too are decorative, with an ornate bridge crossing the overflow for the reservoir. The ponds, which were once purely practical installations for the works, are now used for breeding trout to stock the lake for fishermen. In season, fly fishermen can be seen around the water's edge or casting their lines from boats out on the water. Beyond the engine houses is a shallow stone staircase, while to the right is the more stark concrete of the dam itself.

SHADY STREAMS

The walk now leaves the road for a footpath along the shore of the lake, and across the water is a better view of the black and white fishermen's lodge. The banks are wooded, but there are still good views up ahead as the ground rises up in a series of humps and hillocks.

There is a great variety of bird life for, apart from the water fowl out on the lake, there is also the often noisy population of the woods, which echo to the harsh chatter of magpies and the sharp drumming of woodpeckers.

The path takes on many of the characteristics of a country lane, separated from the fields by a hedgerow that is bright with dog roses in summer. A thin line of trees,

oak and conifer, occupy the narrow strip of land between the path and the water's edge.

At the far end of the lake, as it starts to narrow, its character begins to change. Tall reeds fringe the shore and grow in the shallow water, providing an ideal nesting area for moorhen. Dark, shaded streams splash down the hillside into the lake and these are popular fishing grounds for heron. Willow have crowded round the end of the lake to surround attractive pools where reeds and water lilies flourish.

WOODLAND INTERVAL

The path now deserts the lake and turns off through fields to an area of woodland, largely consisting of low elder and sycamore from which tall pine trees rise dramatically. The brief woodland interval ends with a return to the fields, which includes a passage through an arch created by

▲ This wooden carving of St Matthew appears at the end of a pew in St Andrew's Church, Blagdon (left). The church tower can be seen from the other side of the lake.

dog rose in the hedge. The lake is no longer in view, but you can see the start of the Mendip Hills. The footpath ends at the hamlet of West Town, and the walk continues on country lanes. To the left is a high bank, topped by a hedgerow through which tall trees have grown to spread their branches over the road, while to the right a lower bank and hedge is brightly speckled with flowers during the summer months.

As the road turns to go downhill there is a good viewpoint ❿ over the lake to Blagdon, where the church tower is a prominent landmark, while the Mendips rise up in the background. Along the way there are a number of attractive stone houses, among them Rose Cottage, which has a traditional cottage garden and an unusual porch with a balcony above.

The road returns to the water where the marshy, reedy margin has created an ideal habitat for water fowl. At the end of the road, a signpost still carries the initials SCC, a reminder that although this is now Avon it was once Somerset. Now the walk leaves the road for a footpath through the fields on a path that closely follows the roadway used by fishermen.

It is interesting to compare the farm pasture land, uniformly green, with the untouched meadow between the road and the lake, which is a mass of wild flowers. Although the lake is very close, it is often lost from view behind small copses. Up ahead the view is dominated by the vast modern barns of the farm. Once past these, the path heads steeply uphill towards Blagdon. Near the top of the hill, the path runs into a deep lane surrounded by trees that meet overhead to create a dark green tunnel.

The Pump Room

When work began on Blagdon Reservoir in 1899, four steam engines were ordered to pump the water for the Bristol Waterworks Company. These giant engines were installed in two engine houses with a massive red-brick chimney between — the latter is still impressive even though 50 feet (15 metres) has been taken off the top.

In 1949 electric pumps took over the work, but one of the engine houses still has its magnificent original engines that first began work in 1905. These are beam engines. The beams themselves, high up at the top of the house, weigh 17 tons (16.7 tonnes) each.

With each single stroke of the pistons, the pump delivered 107 gallons (481 litres) of water. In a working day, with three engines working and one on standby, millions of gallons of water were sent on their way to the taps of Bristol. These huge engines did a lot of work, but consumed a vast amount of fuel. Over 8 tons (7.8 tonnes) of coal were burned every day and a special railway was built to Blagdon to keep the boilers at work. Parties can book to see the two remaining engines. One is driven by electricity to show how it would have looked in operation. There are regular open days for visitors.

One of these electric pumps in Blagdon Pumping Station does almost double the work of one of the original beam engines. The diameter of the flywheel is 20 feet (6 metres).

▶*In the event of a flood, water could be carried safely downstream along Blagdon Lake's overflow channel, ultimately draining into the River Yeo. The overflow weir measures 161 feet (48 metres) and is built at the northern end of the dam. Part of the route around the lake includes woodland paths (left).*

LITTLETON-UPON-SEVERN

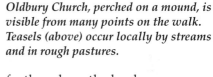

◀ *The red roof and square tower of Oldbury Church, perched on a mound, is visible from many points on the walk. Teasels (above) occur locally by streams and in rough pastures.*

Along the bank of the broad River Severn and across fields to a hamlet

The first section of the route leads alongside the River Severn. Once you are on top of the flood bank **Ⓐ**, a wide vista opens out. Ahead and to your left is the river itself, with the high hills of Wales beyond it. At low tide, the wide expanse of Oldbury Sands is uncovered. This leaves a narrow channel, known as Oldbury Channel, near the shore. Between the flood bank and the water is an area of flat grassland, which is often flooded when the tide is high — the waters of the Severn can rise and fall by as much as 50 feet (15m). To the south is the graceful span of the suspension bridge and, to the north, the rather less graceful outline of Oldbury Nuclear Power Station.

The muddy banks and tidal waters are popular with waders and seabirds, while herons can occasionally be spotted by the streams on the landward side of the bank. A little

further along the bank you can see what looks like a hurdle fence standing in the water at right angles to the shore. This is a 'salmon catch' **Ⓑ**, a traditional means of capturing salmon as they make their way up the narrow channel.

Inland, to the right, is the prominent landmark of Oldbury Church. It has a bright-red tiled roof and is perched on top of a hummocky hill. This section of the walk comes to an end at Oldbury Pill **Ⓒ** — 'pill' is a local name for a tidal inlet. The creek is filled with boats; mainly dinghies, but a few grander yachts as well.

HEADING INLAND

The path turns inland to follow the creek and passes the paddocks of a riding school, then on to the road near the Anchor Inn, on the outskirts of Oldbury-on-Severn. The quiet country lane passes a little stone-built school, where a plaque announces that its erection in 1854 was funded by voluntary contribution and a government grant.

Beyond the school is the attractive Oldbury Church **Ⓓ**, whose nave and aisles are all that remain of the original 13th-century building. In 1897, the church was devastated by fire, but it was sensitively rebuilt to

FACT FILE

✳ Littleton-upon-Severn, 12 miles (19km) north of Bristol

📇 Pathfinders 1131 (ST 49/59) and 1132 (ST 69/79), grid reference ST 588910

miles 0 1 2 3 4 5 6 7 8 9 10 miles
kms 0 1 2 3 4 5 6 7 8 9 10 11 12 13 14 15 kms

◔ Allow 2½ hours

▭ Flat and along good paths

Ⓟ At end of dead-end road signposted to Whale Wharf

🍴 Inn and shop at Littleton; inn at Oldbury

◀ *This stone-built, 17th-century farmhouse was constructed with small windows in order to keep the heat in.*

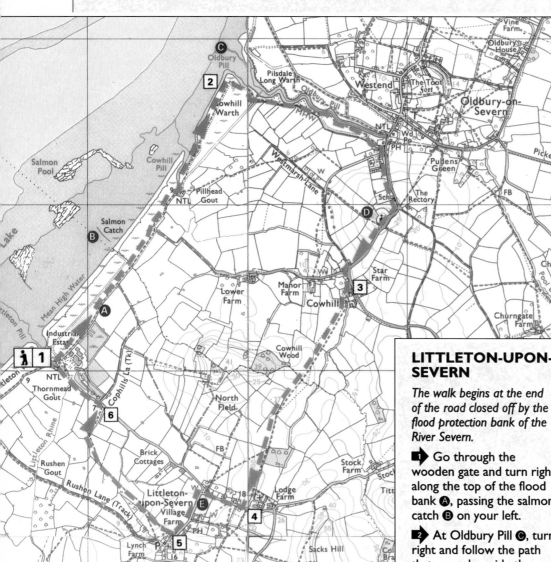

creek. At the road, turn right to Oldbury Church **D**. After visiting the church, continue along the road.

3 Immediately beyond the farmhouse offering cider for sale, turn right through the gate signposted 'Footpath to Littleton 1 mile'. Once over the stile, bear left to leave the orchard by another stile. Continue following the path at the edge of the field. Where the broad farm track swings left to go through the hedge, continue straight on, following the path beside a small wood.

4 Turn right at the road. At the next junction, turn left for Littleton-upon-Severn **E**.

5 Immediately past the White Hart Inn, turn right at the 'Public Footpath' sign. Where the hedge bends round to the right, follow it and continue in that direction.

6 At the road, turn left to return to the start of the walk.

LITTLETON-UPON-SEVERN

The walk begins at the end of the road closed off by the flood protection bank of the River Severn.

1 Go through the wooden gate and turn right along the top of the flood bank **A**, passing the salmon catch **B** on your left.

2 At Oldbury Pill **C**, turn right and follow the path that runs alongside the

retain its essential simplicity. The church has several 18th-century tombstones, decorated with rather chubby but attractive angels.

The road takes you past a farm advertising 'Cowhill cider'. Just beyond a plank bridge, an old cider-press can be seen. The simple screw press is used to extract the juice from apples and this is then fermented to make cider. A path leads off past the farmhouse and through the orchard that supplies the cider-makers with their raw material. The next part of the walk is along footpaths, which lead you across fields and past a little wooded knoll.

Finally, you emerge at the outskirts of Littleton-upon-Severn **E**. You come out by a small, plain church. At the roadway, the first of a number of old stone-built farms

comes into view. The first one is the grandest, with its high gables and small windows topped by drip mouldings that are typical of 16th- and 17th-century design. Beyond it is a small, triangular green, with an old, hand-operated water pump mounted on a brick base.

Soon the road turns to pass the 16th-century White Hart Inn, with its inviting garden. From here, the way continues across the fields,

some of which show the typical 'corrugated' pattern of the medieval ploughed field, though they have been grassed over. The way is crossed by a succession of drainage ditches. There are good views across the river to a patchwork of small fields on the gentle hills on the Welsh side. The final section, along the road, goes past a tree-shaded pond, before returning to the flood bank of the Severn.

▶ *From Oldbury Church there is a fine view of the majestic Severn Bridge, the toll bridge which carries the M4 motorway across the river to Wales.*

DOWN GOBLIN COMBE

◄*This thatched cottage is at the end of the woodland path through Tap's Combe, which is flanked by banks and walls. Wild marjoram (inset) grows in the area on dry, chalky grassland.*

A secluded woodland walk on the outskirts of Bristol

Just outside Bristol, close to the city's airport, is a wooded area cut by clefts with rocky-sided walls. This walk explores this unusual scenery and ends with a stroll across parkland and fields.

The route begins just off the busy A370, down a by-road from the village of Cleeve. It goes past the old school, now a teachers' centre, with its separate entrances for Boys and Girls. An old stone-built farmhouse, Walnut Tree Farm, hides behind a high wall, and is surrounded by outbuildings, one of which has an attractive Pegasus weather vane.

DECIDUOUS TREES

The path narrows as it plunges into dense, broadleaved woodland, through which there are glimpses of pale, shining limestone. In among the slender birch and oak trees are a number of massive beech trees, whose widely spread branches create their own clearings.

The path soon becomes very stony. Cliff faces can be seen rising among the trees, and yew trees have knotted their roots into complex patterns among the rocks. Tongues of scree can be seen licking down the slope to the left and the cliffs become ever higher.

This is Goblin Combe **Ⓐ**, a popular area with rock climbers. It has a

distinctly remote air, and it is hard to believe you are just a mile (1.6km) away from the end of the runway at Bristol Airport. The lower part of the combe, where water drains down from the slopes, becomes very muddy in wet weather. The route climbs to drier ground, leaving the deciduous woodland for an area that contains mostly conifers.

OUT OF THE COMBE

The rocky combe is eventually left behind and you join a grassy track through an avenue of pine trees. The path then turns to go steeply downhill to the road at the end of Brockley Combe. At the roadway is a small quarry surrounded by woods, dominated by a number of old and majestic beech trees.

Soon you leave the road and join a stony path **Ⓑ**, an old route passing between crumbling stone walls. Underfoot, the earth has been worn away to create a pavement of limestone. The path runs partly through and partly at the edge of the woods.

The final section through the woods is downhill. Again, this is an old path, bordered by banks and walls. It ends at the road, by a

▼*These red deer are part of a herd which is farmed for the table at Manor Farm near Brockley Hall.*

FACT FILE

- ❋ Cleeve, 8½ miles (13.6km) south-west of Bristol on the A370

- ▱ Pathfinder 1182 (ST 46/56), grid reference ST 458653

  miles 0 1 2 3 4 5 6 7 8 9 10 miles
  kms 0 1 2 3 4 5 6 7 8 9 10 11 12 13 14 15 kms

- ◔ Allow 3 hours

- ▭ Some very muddy sections in wet weather

- P Car park at the start

- T Served by buses running between Bristol and Weston-super-Mare; Tel. (0117) 9553231

- 🍺 Pub at Cleeve

THE WALL

CLEEVE – GOBLIN COMBE

Begin at the car park by the disused quarry in Cleeve Hill Road, off the A370.

1 Turn right down Plunder Street, past the old school. At the entrance to Walnut Tree Farm, turn right through a gate to join a footpath through Goblin Combe **A**. Continue on the path, keeping to the valley bottom.

2 Shortly after entering an area of conifer woodland, the path divides. Continue following the main path round to the left. Where the path divides again, continue straight on.

A grassy track joins from the right and the broad track swings round to the left. Continue straight on, crossing another track to take the narrower footpath through the woods. The path reaches a clearing by a Public Bridleway sign, where six ways meet.

3 Ignore the first two turnings to the left and continue straight on along the broad path. Continue on this path, ignoring the forest tracks that cross it.

4 At a road, turn right,

then right again on to a larger road leading past a quarry. Just after a sign to Willis's Batch, take a stony path **B** left through the trees. Continue for 550 yards (500m).

5 Where tracks cross, turn left. At the end of a clearing, turn right on a crossing path, downhill through woods.

6 When you reach a lane turn left to reach a main road. Cross the road and turn right. Go left over a stile by a Public Footpath

sign, to walk through parkland **C**. Follow the path round the edge of the woodland as indicated by yellow arrows.

7 At a roadway, turn left, then immediately right to cross a stile into fields. Follow this path past Brockley Court, on your right, and over a road, for about 1¼ miles (2km) to a second road.

8 Turn left. At the main road, turn right, then beyond the garage turn left down Cleeve Hill Road.

delightful thatched cottage with a pretty cottage garden. Ponies graze in the surrounding fields, but the peaceful walk is now briefly interrupted by the busy main road.

The other side of the road presents a contrasting scene of pastoral peace. The route takes you through

part of the old estate of Brockley Hall **C**, a grand house visible over to the left, while the walk itself skirts the wall. On the right is Manor Farm, which raises deer for venison.

The path crosses in front of Brockley Hall's imposing gateway, flanked by lions holding heraldic

shields, before returning to the fields and a splendid sweet chestnut tree.

Another imposing house, Brockley Court, comes into view, with a church alongside it. The route passes in front of the house to continue over fields, then follows roads back to the start of the walk.

AVON

Downland with an isolated feel, right on Bath's doorstep

▲ *The view back to Bristol from the hills east of North Stoke. At many points on the walk the skylark (inset) can be heard singing as it rises far overhead in its song flight.*

This walk explores Lansdown, an exposed, lonely down above the city of Bath. Along the route, you follow part of a long distance footpath, the Cotswold Way, passing through a remote village and a Civil War battleground. There are fine views in all directions; across the Avon and Severn Valleys to the south and west, towards the Wiltshire Downs in the east, and along the Cotswold Edge to the north. A pair of binoculars are an asset, but there is plenty to see without them.

REBUILT PUB

The walk begins at the Blathwayt Arms **A**. The pub stands on the site of the Star Inn, rebuilt after World War II and renamed after William Blathwayt, Secretary of State to William and Mary, who once owned much of Lansdown.

Behind is Bath Race Course **B**, which moved to its present location

---

FACT FILE

* Lansdown, 3 miles (4.8km) north-west of Bath

* Pathfinders 1183 (ST 66/76) and 1167 (ST 67/77), grid reference ST 725686

miles 0 1 2 3 4 5 6 7 8 9 10 miles
kms 0 1 2 3 4 5 6 7 8 9 10 11 12 13 14 15 kms

* Allow 3 hours

* One long steady ascent, otherwise fairly level walking on field paths and tracks. Several sections may be muddy or stony. Walking boots recommended

* P Blathwayt Arms car park

* T Park and ride bus from Bath to Lansdown, Mon–Fri

* The Blathwayt Arms in Lansdown serves food

---

in 1830. Previously, races were run between Beckford's Tower, still a prominent landmark to the south-east, and Lansdown Lane. The Bath Races were popular during the Regency (1810-20), when the prestigious Bath Cup was worth the vast sum of 100 guineas. Nowadays, there are ten days of flat racing a year.

At other times, parts of the course are used for grazing cattle or walking dogs, and by model airplane enthusiasts. The liquid song of the skylark is frequently heard over the racecourse, although the bird itself is not easy to spot.

Across the racecourse is the viewpoint of Prospect Stile **C**, complete with a toposcope. Bath is laid out to

THE WALK

LANSDOWN – NORTH STOKE – HANGING HILL

The walk begins from the car park of the Blathwayt Arms **Ⓐ**.

1 Step over the rail at the left end of the pub. At the end of the wall, turn right onto a path between the wall and the running rail of the racecourse. The path narrows and goes behind the grandstand of Bath Race Course **Ⓑ**. Bear left around the buildings onto a rutted track. Go through a gap in the running rail and across the race course. After 25 yards

(22m), take an ill-defined track half-right. Keep ahead, making for the right-hand end of the trees on the near horizon. Cross the racecourse again. There is a section of rail

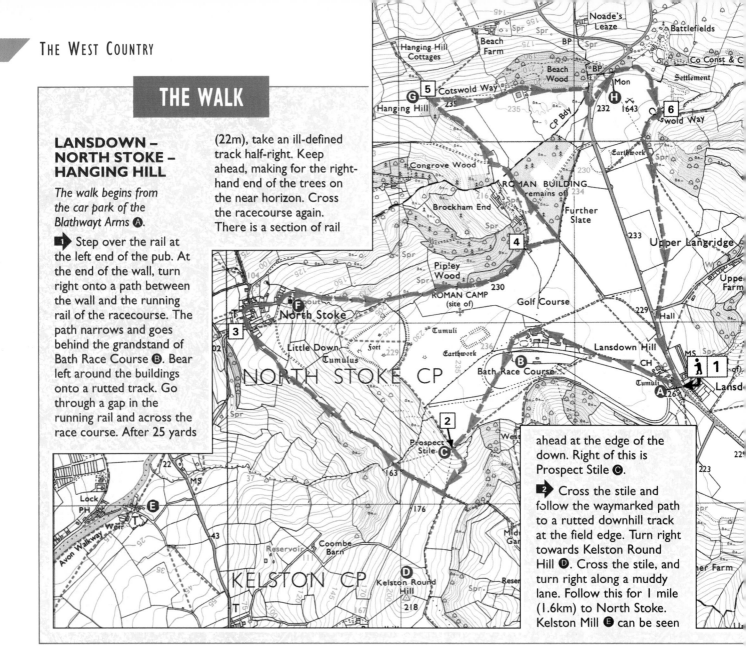

ahead at the edge of the down. Right of this is Prospect Stile **Ⓒ**.

2 Cross the stile and follow the waymarked path to a rutted downhill track at the field edge. Turn right towards Kelston Round Hill **Ⓓ**. Cross the stile, and turn right along a muddy lane. Follow this for 1 mile (1.6km) to North Stoke. Kelston Mill **Ⓔ** can be seen

the left of the stile, with the abbey, the university and Sham Castle making good reference points. Bristol is to the right; binoculars will pick out Brunel's suspension bridge at Clifton. On the far horizon ahead, beyond the villages and towns of the Avon Valley, is Beacon Batch, the highest point on the Mendips.

You descend on the Cotswold Way towards the local landmark of Kelston Round Hill **Ⓓ**. The Cotswold Way is not a purpose-made long distance path; it was created by linking existing rights-of-way, and stretches almost 100 miles (160km) from Bath to Chipping Campden.

QUIET PASTURES

Before reaching the hill, you turn off along a muddy lane between fields, which contours the side of the hill. There are quiet pastures above, while to the left there is far more activity. A motocross track serpentines muddily across the lower slopes, and, at weekends, the guns of clay pigeon shoots mingle with the raucous cries of birds from the local rookery.

◀*The walk crosses Bath Race Course, which hosts some ten days of exciting flat racing during the year.*

in the distance on the left.

3 Turn right along the road, and follow it to St Martin's Church **F**. Go up the steps to visit the church, then back down and right between the farm and the churchyard. Bear right past a barn, and through a gate to a rutted track. Follow this uphill for 600 yards (540m). Continue through a gate and straight ahead to a building on your right.

4 Turn right, then left at a crossing track, with a wood on your right. At the end of the wood, continue bearing left downhill on the track. At a gate, climb the bank to your right and go through a gap in the wall. Walk between the wall and a line of conifers to a stile. Cross and keep straight ahead to the trig point at Hanging Hill **G**.

5 Cross the stile, and turn right along the fence. Go ahead through a gate, and along a narrow path by a radio mast to a surfaced

track. Turn right. After a short distance, go left on a tarmac drive and follow it as it bends right just before the road. Turn left at the Cotswold Way signpost, across the road to a stile. The Lansdown Monument **H** is straight ahead. Pass to the right of the monument, descend a little way, then turn right over a stile and around two sides of a field. Climb the stone steps over the wall ahead.

6 The Cotswold Way is signposted downhill to the left, but you turn right along the line of the wall. Go through a waymarked gate, and over the stile ahead. Turn right along the field edge, then left at the fence. Keep ahead through two gates. At the third gate, by a barn, bear half-right to a building and a stand of trees. Between the two is a stile onto a road. Cross and go straight ahead up an access road. Bear left at the main road to return to the start.

▲ *On the approach to North Stoke there are views down to the old annealing ovens by the weir at Kelston Mill. In North Stoke itself the walk passes St Martin's Church (below).*

brassworks at nearby Warmley were the largest in the world at the time.

Ahead and to the left, the view is dominated by the massive, red-brick Cadbury's chocolate factory at Keynsham, with south Bristol stretching away behind.

At the end of the lane is the secluded village of North Stoke. This ancient place is thought to have been continuously occupied for

◄ *As you descend from Prospect Stile the view ahead is dominated by the tree-topped mound of Kelston Round Hill.*

Gaps in the tangle of thorns and ivy-covered trees that line the way reveal views over the Avon Valley. In the middle distance is the weir at Kelston Mill **E**, a reminder of the region's once thriving brass industry. This made use of calamine (a zinc ore) from the Mendips and coal from the mines of Kingswood Forest to the west. The tall, truncated pyramids that you can see are annealing ovens, all that is left of William Champion's brass foundry, built around 1760. Champion's

approximately 2,500 years. The site of the original Celtic village is on a high, sheltered spot on the shoulder of the hill. Today, it is a place of mellow stone decorated with lichen and red pantile roofs. Particularly noteworthy is Manor Farm's Georgian shell-hood over its front door.

WONDERFUL VIEWS

At the top of the village is St Martin's Church **F**. The inside is unassuming, though there are interesting wall tablets. Outside, a spring drops through pools, and there are fine views from the churchyard.

Back on the Cotswold Way, you embark on a long, steady climb up a rutted path lined with mossy oaks supporting straggles of wild clematis. Rabbits are abundant on the slopes to your left. Below are the scattered houses of Pipley Bottom. There is a real sense of remoteness from the cities of Bath and Bristol.

Back on top of Lansdown, you follow a grassy track between a golf course and a wood which clings to the slopes behind a crumbling stone wall. The path winds on around the edge of the down to Hanging Hill **G**. Here, there are views west across the plain, dotted with stone-built villages and country houses, to the hills of Wales. The Cotswold scarp stretches away to the north.

LANSDOWN MONUMENT

You pass a Ministry of Defence installation, and cross the road to the Lansdown Monument **H**. This was erected in 1720 to the memory of Bevil Grenvile, killed very near this spot at the Battle of Lansdown

▲*As the path climbs to Hanging Hill there is a view across Pipley Bottom to North Stoke and Keynsham.*

in 1643. The column has trophies and coats of arms carved in relief, and is topped by a griffin. The monument, now protected by a railing, is etched with graffiti from the 18th and 19th centuries.

CHARMY DOWN

The path skirts a large field where much of the fighting took place; the Royalists made their charge up the steep, wooded slopes to your left. You leave the Cotswold Way as it drops down into a lovely, bowl-like valley, with splendid views across to Charmy Down, site of a disused airfield, and the Wiltshire hills rolling away to the horizon. From here, it is a short walk across farmland back to the Blathwayt Arms.

A Doubtful Victory

In the autumn of 1642, Charles I planned a campaign to wrest London from the Roundheads. While forces from the west and north converged on the capital, cutting off supply lines and blocking the Thames, he intended to hold up the Parliamentary troops in Oxford.

A charismatic Cornishman, Sir Bevil Grenvile, raised an army of almost 1,500 well-disciplined and well-armed men in the West. They fought with such success in Sir Ralph Hopton's Royalist army that Cromwell sent Sir William Waller, one of his best generals, to head off their advance at Bath. Hopton and Waller had been good friends before the war, when, ironically, they had often met at Bath.

The Royalists first marched on the

In the Civil War Battle of Lansdown (below left), which was fought to prevent the Royalists advancing on Bath, Cromwell's Roundhead troops were led by the renowned general, William Waller (above).

city via Frome and Bradford-on-Avon, but Waller stopped their progress along the river valley. Hopton's men took to the hills at Marshfield, intending to launch an assault on Bath from above. On 5 July 1643, the two armies met in battle at Lansdown.

Waller planted his cannon on an almost inaccesible piece of ground on the north-western side of the ridge. Seeing their foe so well established, the Royalists considered retreating, but the irrepressible Cornish infantry led a frontal charge over Waller's breastworks.

Technically, the Royalists won the day, but more than half the Cornish army, including Sir Bevil, were lost, and Waller, though forced to retreat, managed to hang on to Bath.

▲*Carved into Bevil Grenvile's Lansdown Monument are the initials of 18th-century visitors.*

A PROSPECT OF WALES

▲South-westerly winds, blowing across the Bristol Channel, have shaped coastal trees into arches. Navelwort, or wall pennywort (above right), grows from banks and walls on the route.

FACT FILE

⚹ Portishead, 9 miles (14.4km) west of Bristol, on the A369

⬛ Pathfinder 1166 (ST 47/57), grid reference ST 439751

miles 0 1 2 3 4 5 6 7 8 9 10 miles
kms 0 1 2 3 4 5 6 7 8 9 10 11 12 13 14 15 kms

◗ Allow at least 3 hours

▬ Generally easy walking, with two short, steep ascents. Rough underfoot in places. Stout shoes or boots are required

P The Ship pub car park at the start

T Regular bus service from Bristol

🏠 Several pubs and cafés in Portishead. Pub at Weston in Gordano

I For Tourist Information, Tel. (01934) 626838

Ancient sites and a crusader's tomb by the Severn Estuary

Portishead, on a commanding position on a ridge above the Severn Estuary, is recorded in the *Domesday Book* as a small community of about a dozen men, its lands and buildings valued at 70 shillings. At that time, it was at the head of a peninsula; the low-lying land to the south and east, part of the Somerset Levels, had not been drained.

In recent times, the town has centred on its docks and industries. The tide at Portishead rises and falls more than 40 feet (12m), the second largest differential in the world. Two power stations built here between the World Wars have made use of this factor in their cooling systems.

This walk looks at the country to the south-west of the town, along the line of the ridge. The route winds down through the residential streets of Redcliff Bay (note the unusual method of identifying No. 74 Hillside Road, at the junction with Waterside Gardens) to the clifftop coast path Ⓐ.

NATURAL ARCHWAYS

Prevailing south-west winds sweep along the coast, and some of the trees and hedges make archways across the path. Among the many plants flowering in the shelter of the hedgerows are red and white campion and navelwort.

There are fine views across the estuary and the Bristol Channel. At low tide, massive golden-brown sandbanks are left high and dry. South Wales appears as a faint, shimmering haze across the muddy waters, which are usually busy with craft both large and small.

Just beyond the signal station, the route leaves the coast to climb onto

▼*The view from Walton Common Down towards wooded Court Hill.*

THE WALK

REDCLIFF BAY – WALTON IN GORDANO

The walk starts from the lower car park of The Ship pub, on the junction of Down Road and Hillside Road, at the south-western end of Portishead.

1 Go down Hillside Road, which zigzags, then turn left into Waterside Park, a cul-de-sac. Go straight ahead to a path between the houses, which leads to the coast path **A**.

2 Turn left and follow the path for 1½ miles (2.4km). Continue uphill for about 400 yards (360m) beyond the Signal Station to a stile into a field on the left.

3 Cross the stile and continue uphill with the hedge/wall on your left to a gate and stile. Ignore the footpath sign right and go ahead to a second stile, onto a road. Turn right and follow the road until you reach a 'Road Narrows' sign on your right.

4 Take the footpath left, opposite the sign. Climb to Walton Common Down **B**, bearing left through woods to a saucer-shaped scar of rough stones in the centre of the down. Continue

over the down in the same general direction, bearing gradually left to pick up a wide, grassy track that leads to an earth track through Common Hill Wood. Follow this track to a T-junction marked by a white post with yellow arrows. Turn right and follow this track to a stile.

5 Cross and turn left. Continue along the top of this field and the next, with woods on your left. At the corner of the second field, turn right and follow the fence on your left down to a road. Turn left to the Church of St Peter and St Paul **C** at Weston in Gordano. Continue through the village and turn left into Hill Lane opposite the White Hart. Continue to the end of the lane.

6 Take the footpath uphill and shortly fork right through the trees, to emerge above a fenced area. Continue uphill to join a gravelled lane, then emerge into Valley Road.

7 Continue down Valley Road and turn left at the bottom to reach the start.

Walton Common Down **B**. This rough pasture on the summit of the ridge, enclosed by trees, was once common grazing land of Walton in Gordano, which lies down the hill to the south. It contains many ancient sites including hut circles, field systems, an enclosure and a tumulus, but none of these are easy to see from the ground.

It is possible to sit here unaware of the outside world, save for the noise of the nearby M5 percolating occasionally through the trees. Patience may be rewarded by the sight of a buzzard, a hovering kestrel or a silent owl at dusk; the huge rabbit population here provides a ready source of food.

The route goes through woods and fields to the village of Weston in Gordano. In the Church of St Peter and St Paul **C**, founded in the 11th century, is the tomb of Sir Richard de Perceval, who travelled with King Richard I on the Third Crusade to the Holy Land. Sir Richard lost an arm and a leg in combat, but continued to ride into battle, his sword in his hand and the reins of his horse between his teeth. Despite his handicaps he lived to return to England.

PRIME MINISTER'S CROSS

Another member of his family is commemorated in the churchyard. A cross was erected in 1910 in memory of Spencer Perceval, Prime Minister from 1809 to 1812. In that year he was shot dead in the House of Commons lobby by a merchant, John Bellingham, who blamed the government for his own bankruptcy. Perceval is the only British Prime Minister to have been assassinated. From Weston, there is a climb up and over the ridge to return to the starting point of the walk.

▶ *The Church of St Peter and St Paul, where Spencer Perceval, who dreamt of his assassination, is commemorated.*

AVON

◄*Just off the route, in the village of Stanton Drew, the three Cove Stones were put in place at least 4,000 years ago. The bream (inset) is a coarse fish that can be found in the River Chew.*

until 1958, and was the first in Britain to have pithead baths.

The route goes under the viaduct into the town of Pensford, where it crosses the river on an old stone bridge. Its modern concrete equivalent carries the A37, which divides the village, over the Chew a little further downstream.

You pass by the now somewhat dilapidated church. Note Bridge House, built on an arch over the river, and Mill Corner, the site of the old town mill. A mark on the corner records the flood level of 1968, when the waters of the Chew rose over head-height in the street.

While the path into Pensford was at low level by the river, the one leaving it climbs a grassy knoll. There are views over the undulating

An impressive prehistoric monument in a lovely river valley

The River Chew runs through a rolling rural landscape a few miles south of Bristol, in what was once north Somerset. Several ancient sites lie along its course. This walk visits the best of them, and exlores some interesting villages.

It begins at Upper Stanton Drew, on a footpath that runs by a shady lane. A tiny stone footbridge with pointed arches takes the walk over a brook towards a line of trees that marks the course of the River Chew.

The river, a gentle, reedy stream, leads to what looks from a distance to be a brick house, but is actually built of bright-red sandstone. Here, the river divides, sluices Ⓐ diverting some of its water to the mill at Pensford. The mill originally ground corn, but was later adapted for the manufacture of copper and brass.

The path goes slightly uphill, and at the top a view opens out towards a majestic, 16-arch viaduct Ⓑ that once carried the railway branch line from Bristol to Radstock.

PITHEAD BATHS

To the right is a scrubby hillside, quite unlike the smooth, grassy swells all around. This is an overgrown spoil heap from Pensford Pit, which was a working coal mine

FACT FILE

- ✳ Upper Stanton Drew, 8 miles (12.8km) west of Bath, north of the A368

- Pathfinders 1182 (ST 46/56) and 1183 (ST 66/76), grid reference ST 603628

  miles 0 1 2 3 4 5 6 7 8 9 10 miles
  kms 0 1 2 3 4 5 6 7 8 9 10 11 12 13 14 15 kms

- ◖ Allow 2½ hours

- One fairly steep climb. Field paths can be muddy, and overgrown in summer. Walking boots are recommended

- P On street in Upper Stanton Drew; wide roadway near Stanton Wick Lane

- T Hourly buses from Bristol to Pensford, Tel. (0117) 9553231.
- I Tourist Information, Tel. (0117) 9260767
- Pubs and shops in Stanton Drew and Pensford
- Stanton Drew Circles; Tel. (0117) 9750700 for further details

THE WALK

UPPER STANTON DREW – PENSFORD – NORTON MALREWARD

The walk begins in Upper Stanton Drew, by the start of Stanton Wick Lane.

▶ By an 'Unsuitable for Heavy Goods Vehicles' sign is a path marked 'Avon Cycle Way'. Follow it to where the road turns right by a little arched bridge.

▶ Turn left to cross the stile by a public footpath sign. Follow the hedge down to the river, and follow the river round past some sluices Ⓐ to a viaduct Ⓑ. The path is marked by yellow arrows. Walk under the viaduct towards the farm.

▶ At a road, turn left and cross the bridge over the river. Immediately beyond the Rising Sun Inn, take the footpath to the right of the stone building.

▶ Beyond the viaduct, the path divides. Turn right onto the path beside the telegraph poles. Follow the hedge

on your right, and continue uphill past an oak tree. At a copse, keep right over a metal gate and head towards an iron shed. Cross the stile to the left of the shed. Go through the house yard to a road.

▶ Turn left, then immediately right. At the junction with the main

road, take the path left to Belluton Farm. Continue uphill, keeping a barn to your left, towards a stile.

▶ At the top of Settle Hill Ⓒ, bear slightly left and head towards the right-hand pylon visible on the horizon (this field may be planted with crops, with no clear

path). When you see the church at Norton Malreward up ahead, follow the track down towards it.

▶ At the road, turn left. Ignore a turning to your right. At a second junction, turn right, then right again at a T-junction. Turn left by the toll-house Ⓓ.

▶ Beyond a bridge, the road divides. Follow the path to the left, signposted to the stone circles Ⓔ. Take the track signposted 'Two Rivers Public Footpath', waymarked with yellow arrows. At the road, turn right to walk back to the start.

countryside as you climb to the top of Settle Hill Ⓒ, a broad plateau of tall grass and clover, with a magnificent prospect out to the Mendips.

The descent takes you to Norton Malreward, which has a little church

◀This tall brick viaduct once carried the Bristol to Radstock branch line.

with a square tower, and next to it a magnificent Georgian house, Manor Farm. At the roadway, the route passes the house of an enthusiastic collector of old enamelled signs, which cover every inch of the wall. Peaceful lanes lead down to a pretty little valley with a brook and a hillside of copses, where green woodpeckers can be seen and heard.

An unusual hexagonal toll-house Ⓓ with a conical thatched roof stands at the crossroads outside Stanton Drew. An old stone bridge across the River Chew affords a brief glimpse of some of the village's

grander houses before you turn off towards the stone circles Ⓔ.

There are three rings in all, the largest being a true circle about 120 yards (108m) across. The stones are massive, though many have fallen over. They were assembled over 5000 years ago in the New Stone Age, and the whole site covered a large area, comparable to those at Stonehenge and Avebury.

Many other stones can be found in the village and the surrounding fields. There is a good view from the walk, but, for those who want a closer look, the stones are on private land and a small charge is payable. From here, it is a short walk across fields back to the start.

From Cheddar Gorge into the Mendips

The walk begins at the popular tourist area of Cheddar, well-known for its cheeses, caves and the gorge. The start of the walk leads up to the top of the gorge by Jacob's Tower **B**, built in 1908 so that visitors who climbed Jacob's Ladder **A** could have a good view from the top. It still provides an excellent panorama of the gorge, Cheddar reservoir, the Mendip Hills and the Somerset Levels.

A SPECTACULAR GORGE

Cheddar Gorge **C** is a great cleft in the rocks rising to almost 1000 feet (304 metres) above the road. It was cut by a river thousands of years ago, which then found an easier route underground. Today it emerges only at the end of the gorge. The ancient river has, however, left behind one of the country's most spectacularly deep limestone gorges.

FACT FILE

⚹ Cheddar, Somerset

🚌 Pathfinder 1198 (ST 45/55), grid reference ST 464539

miles 0 1 2 3 4 5 6 7 8 9 10 miles
kms 0 1 2 3 4 5 6 7 8 9 10 11 12 13 14 15 kms

◔ Allow 3½ hours

◣ Steep and stony in places, and downhill slopes muddy in winter. Wear good walking shoes

🅿 On the B3235 at Cheddar. The most convenient car park is opposite the entrance to Jacob's Ladder, but others are available nearby

🚍 Badger Line buses run from Wells and Weston-super-Mare

🏛🍽 Refreshments and toilets available at Cheddar

▲ *The wooded limestone cliffs of the gorge. (inset) Cheddar pinks are rare wild flowers found in the cliffs.*
▼ *Jacob's Tower overlooks the gorge.*

The river also scooped out the magnificent cave system of 400 caverns for which Cheddar is famous. Walkers should, however, note that the gorge is precipitous and they should be very careful when approaching the rim.

From the highest point of the gorge, the walk continues as a well-defined track through the bracken and shrubs, then joins the West Mendip Way just before going steeply downhill through woodland. After crossing the main road, the path enters the Somerset Trust for Nature Conservation Reserve. There are a number of waymarked trails in the area, and various leaflets are available from a box by the signboard.

THE WALK

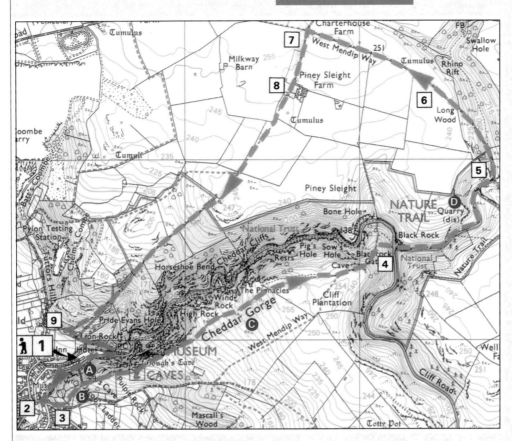

CHEDDAR GORGE

The start is in the car park at Cheddar, next to the hotel and opposite the entrance to Jacob's Ladder Ⓐ.

1 From the car park turn right on to the main road, away from the gorge.

2 At the road junction, turn left, opposite the garage, and take the narrow road, the further left of the two, leading uphill.

3 Take the next left turning. The path immediately divides. Turn left through the wooden gate on to the bridleway. This leads uphill past Jacob's Tower Ⓑ to the top of the gorge Ⓒ. Just before running steeply downhill through scrubby woodland, it joins up with the West Mendip Way.

4 At the road, cross straight over to the stile on the opposite side. Be careful as the road can be busy. Continue, following the wide track past the limekiln Ⓓ, ignoring footpaths through the woods to the right.

5 Where the path divides, with a stile on the right, continue following the main track round to the left. Cross the next stile and where the path divides, follow the path indicated by the yellow arrow to Shipham, to the left.

6 At the edge of the woodland cross over a stile and follow the path beside the wall to cross a succession of stiles.

7 A broad, rough farm road crosses the footpath. Turn left across the cattle grid, leaving the West Mendip Way.

8 At the farm, where the track divides, take the path to the right. Cross the stile and continue across the field to the far gate opposite. Continue following the wall, cross the stile, then go downhill on the grassy path, which gradually narrows to run first through scrubland, then over a stile to continue through thicker woods. Ignore all paths to the left.

9 At the houses, turn sharply back to the left on to the narrow pathway. At the gateway and sign 'Public Footpath' turn left on to the broad track.

10 At the main road, turn right to return to car park.

The Black Rock area was once part of a medieval royal hunting ground.

The walk carries on by following the former quarry track with a 200-year-old drystone wall alongside. It reaches the now disused old Black Rock quarry Ⓓ at the foot of which is an old limekiln. In its working days, this was loaded with alternate layers of fuel and stone through the round hole at the top and then allowed to burn for several days. The lime for building and agriculture was taken out through the arched opening at the bottom. The path then becomes a broad grassy track, winding down a lovely, rocky valley, before disappearing briefly into the old coppiced woodland.

Beyond the edge of the woodland, the nature of the walk changes to wide, grassy fields bordered by limestone walls. This pleasantly gentle walk through farmland lasts until the path begins to turn downhill again back to Cheddar, with fine views across the circular lake, Cheddar Reservoir, and with glimpses of the promontories and cliffs of the gorge.

The final part of the walk is down a narrow, stony path that plunges through dense woodland. It is well defined, but could become slippery in wet weather. The path leads back to the edge of the town.

A View from Beacon Hill

Open moors with broad vistas in the Quantock Hills

A contrasting landscape of open heathland and wooded valleys characterises this walk. It leads from the deep cleft of Hodder's Combe to the moorland of Beacon Hill, with its panoramic views, back down to the narrow valley of Smith's Combe and on through fields.

The village of Holford at the start is soon left behind, and the path crosses the footbridge at Hodder's Combe **A**, where a stream rushes and tumbles over a small waterfall.

THE GREAT ROAD

Back on the road, the most obvious feature is a brick enclosure, which was once the local dog pound **B** — an old structure that was made over to the villagers in 1982. This also marks the beginning of the rough, tree-lined track **C** leading to the summit of Longstone Hill. Clearly marked by banks on either side, at times reinforced by dry-stone walls in the typical herring-bone pattern of the region, it is obviously a man-made route.

The first thought is that it might be a drove road, but it was once the Great Road, from Holford to West Quantoxhead, and the route the mail coaches took. Extra horses were laid on for the steep climb and then detached at the top of the hill and led back down again.

As the pathway runs clear of the trees, it reaches open moorland of gorse, heather and bracken, with superb views over the Bristol Channel on a clear day.

This swallow has no time to stop. It takes a much-needed drink on the wing.

▲ *The panoramic views across the fields from the top of Beacon Hill are worth the climb. On a clear day you can see the Welsh coast at the other side of the Bristol Channel. (inset) The Great Road was once the mail route.*

The open moor is criss-crossed with paths and bridleways and is a popular horse-riding area. It is also used by the local stag hunt. Those hoping for a quiet walk should avoid Mondays and Thursdays between the beginning of September and the end of April.

At the brow of the hill, the view opens out to the west across to the wide expanses of Exmoor. The walk culminates at Beacon Hill **D**, at 1,017 feet (310 metres) the highest point in the Quantocks.

The next section of the walk, down Smith's Combe **E**, offers a complete contrast. The way downhill begins as a broad, grassy track and leads into a narrow valley of broad-leaved trees with a little stream. At the end of Smith's

FACT FILE

⚹ Holford, Quantock Hills

🚗 Pathfinder 1216 (ST 04/14), grid reference ST 157413

miles 0 1 2 3 4 5 6 7 8 9 10 miles
kms 0 1 2 3 4 5 6 7 8 9 10 11 12 13 14 15 kms

◔ Allow 2½ hours

▬ Mainly easy going on well-used paths, though a little steep and stony in places. Suitable all year round

P Parking in Holford village near the Plough Inn. Alternatively use car park at Holford Green. The exit leads directly to the old Dog Pound (**4** in the instructions)

T Regular bus service between Minehead and Bridgwater May–Sept, Tel. (01823) 272033

🍴 Refreshments available at Holford

THE WALK

(map of the walk route around East Quantoxhead and Holford, with numbered waypoints 1–13 and lettered points A–E)

HOLFORD-BEACON HILL

The walk starts in the minor road behind the pub, the Plough Inn.

1 At the first left bend, continue past the sign for bridleway.

2 As the road bends left again, turn right over the stile by the public footpath sign, marked with a yellow arrow, and cross the footbridge over the valley of Hodder's Combe **Ⓐ**, climbing up to a minor road.

3 When you reach the roadway turn left.

4 At the old Dog Pound **Ⓑ**, turn right on to the broad track **Ⓒ**, which passes between high banks and woodland. Keep to the broad track and, at the edge of the trees, continue straight on as indicated by the signpost to West Quantoxhead.

5 Where the paths cross, continue straight on following the blue arrow to West Quantoxhead.

6 Where the path divides, take the path to the left. The first objective, the cairn on Beacon Hill, can be seen ahead and to the right.

7 At the crossing of paths, turn right and soon afterwards take the left fork towards the cairn.

8 From the summit of Beacon Hill **Ⓓ**, turn right towards the sea along the track. At the next crossing follow the footpath signposted to Smith's Combe **Ⓔ**.

9 Cross the stream at the foot of the hill and follow the path round to the left.

10 At the edge of the moorland just before the fields, 50 yards (45 metres) in front of a metal gate, take the path to the right, uphill round the shoulder of the hill. Where the path divides take the route to the left, following a line round the hill just above the level of the fields.

11 When you arrive at the roadway turn left.

12 Turn right by the first houses, following the sign to YHA — the track bends round to the right. At the notice saying 'Private Drive to Steepholm and YHA', turn left on path signposted 'Bridleway'. Follow the direction of the blue arrows.

13 At the roadway turn left and continue, to rejoin the footpath at **3** for the return to Holford village.

Combe the path returns to agricultural land as it opens out to give a marvellous view down to the sea, which is now just a mile (1.6 km) away.

Having come almost down to sea level, there is now a short, but sharp climb round the shoulder of the hill. The path then runs through bracken along the dividing line between the farmland that stretches down to the coast on the left and the moorland to the right. The final section leads through fields where, in late summer, it is not unusual to see deer grazing on the remains of harvested cornfields. It ends at a road through the woodland for the return walk to Holford village.

Colourful rhododendrons are a feature of Smith's Combe in May.

INTO AN ENCHANTED GORGE

A varied walk through a deep, wooded gorge to the mysterious sites of Neolithic Man

The walk incorporates the best of Mendip scenery as well as sites of great historic interest. It includes a deep, wooded limestone gorge; a rough upland plateau; pre-historic sites dating back for thousands of years; and the crumbling remains of the once-important lead mines.

The walk begins with a steep descent, eased by steps cut in the

FACT FILE

✴ Ebbor Gorge

🚏 Pathfinders 1198 (ST 45/55) and 1218 (ST 44/54), grid reference ST 520484

miles 0   1   2   3   4   5   6   7   8   9   10 miles
kms 0   1   2   3   4   5   6   7   8   9   10   11   12   13   14   15 kms

🕐 Allow 3½ hours

🔺 The path out of the gorge is rough and steep, and can be slippery in wet weather. North Hill is a narrow path through tussocky grass, so good footwear is necessary

🅿 Ebbor Gorge Car Park

🏠 Two public houses at Priddy with gardens and play areas

▲ *A deep, wooded limestone gorge in the heart of the Ebbor Gorge. Grasshopper warblers (inset), which get their name from the distinctive churring song, can be found nesting in rough grass. The Ebbor Gorge Nature Reserve, Somerset (right).*

path, through woodland to the foot of the Gorge Ⓐ. This valley, carved out by an ancient river, is marked by high limestone cliffs that rear up on both sides of the footpath. The many small caves and rock shelters were once home to animals such as wolves and bears, long since extinct in Britain, and were used by

THE WALK

EBBOR GORGE

The walk starts at the National Trust car park at Ebbor Gorge, which lies on the minor road linking Priddy to Wookey Hole.

1 Leave the car park by the stone stile opposite the entrance and take the path downhill through the woods. Where the path divides turn left.

2 At the next division, turn left following the arrow pointing to The Gorge **A**.

3 At the top of the gorge follow the path round to the right, signposted 'Car Park'.

4 At the next junction turn left and follow the path ahead. The first stile along the path is signposted 'West Mendip Way, Priddy'. At Higher Pitts Farm, follow the footpath through the smaller of the two gates.

5 Follow the metalled farm road to the left then, where it turns left again, turn right on the green pathway between high hedgerows. After 219 yards (200 metres), turn left through the gate into the field. The path now stays close to the wall across the fields.

6 At the road turn right. Those who would prefer a shorter walk can turn left at this stage and follow the road straight on to Priddy **E**. On entering the village turn left at the first lane, which is designated 'single track'. The Queen Victoria Inn is visible a short way down this road. Continue to the outskirts of the village, then follow the instructions from Stage 12.

7 Turn left approximately halfway to the garage up a track marked 'Underbarrow Farm'. The path runs to the left of the disturbed ground of the old mining area **B**.

8 At the pond, a broad track leads round to the right and left of a noticeboard. Do not follow either track, but seek a less distinct path, not visible from the pond, which starts close by near the bottom of a wall. Follow this track uphill, keeping the wall on your left-hand side. At the top of the hill you find the Bronze Age barrows **C**. On passing through the gate by the first set of burial mounds, turn right across the field aiming for the middle of the line of mounds up ahead. From the mound, head for the obvious break in the trees.

9 The gateway leads out on to the road. Cross the road to see the Priddy circles **D**, then cross back and re-enter the field. Turn back taking a line between the line of mounds on the left and the trees on the right.

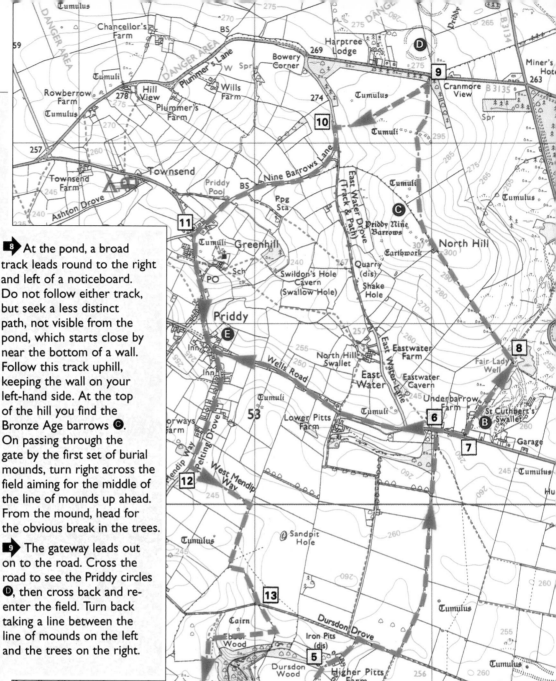

10 At the roadway turn left. Do not take the path marked 'Public Footpath', but keep to the road.

11 At the crossroads turn left on to the road to Priddy **E**. Pass the New Inn on your right, then turn right on to the single track lane towards the Queen Victoria Inn.

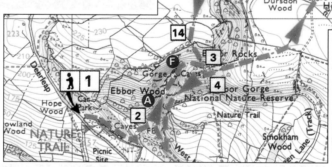

12 Beyond the Priddy sign at the edge of the village, turn left on to a footpath, signposted 'Wookey Hole'. Follow the path around the field to the stile in the opposite corner. Cross over the stone stile in the next wall and follow the wall.

13 At the broad footpath cross straight over and cross the stile opposite. Do not follow the sign indicating a path to Wookey Hole. Follow the path round to the right, over a series of stiles, until you reach a stile on the left into the gorge.

14 Cross the stile and take the footpath downhill into the Gorge, which brings you down to join the path up from the Gorge. At the top of this path, a signpost indicating 'Cliff Top View', leads to a superb vantage point. Continue on, but at Stage 4 on the map turn right following the signpost to the car park at the start.

together with heaps of slag (smelting refuse) from the furnaces.

The walk itself, past the mining site, runs through pine trees, heather and gorse to a small pond. The whole region is so impregnated with lead that only certain plants — Spring Sandwort and Spotted Orchis, for example — will grow here. Rare plants such as these have led to the area being designated one of Special Scientific Interest.

The path now heads uphill through an area of rough, tussocky grass, bracken and gorse. Lead pollution ensures that these lower

◀ *The view from the cliff top above the limestone crags shows the breathtaking beauty of the Ebbor Gorge. The remains of surface buildings at St Cuthbert's lead mine (below), which only ceased production at the beginning of the century.*

Neolithic Man as long ago as 3000 BC. Today, the Gorge offers a splendid walkway, hemmed in by trees and overhanging limestone crags that gradually close in to form a narrow passage through the rocks. The way out at the far end of the Gorge is a rock path through a narrow defile, where the crags seem almost to close in overhead.

ANCIENT MINES

Having climbed out of the Gorge, the path leads on to the edge of the woodland and out on to an area of rough grassland, dotted with gorse bushes. From the top of the hill there are magnificent views out across the flat plain to the Somerset Levels, interrupted by the shapely cone of Glastonbury Tor. An area of disturbed ground near the top of the hill is evidence of former mining activity. Beyond Higher Pitts Farm, the walk continues beside the limestone walls, which are a characteristic feature of the area. Here on the plateau, the meadows are rich and lush with a mixture of grasses and clover.

The route briefly joins the main road before turning off along a footpath with an area of rough, disturbed ground to the right. This is the site of the old St Cuthbert's lead mines ❸. Lead was mined in the Mendips as long ago as Roman times, but the works were abandoned as the ore veins ran out.

Then, in the 19th century, a new technology was introduced that enabled substantial quantities of the metal to be recovered from the previously unproductive spoil heaps.

The remains of these works, which only closed in 1908, can be seen on the other side of the little valley. Furnaces were set up and the waste gases were fed down a series of flues in which the lead condensed: to recover it workers had to crawl the length of the flues scraping the lead deposits off the walls. It was a dangerously unhealthy occupation. Remains of flue systems and surface buildings can still be seen,

slopes remain wild, but near the top of the hill, the fields can be grazed so this area is springy, close-cropped turf. Here is a spectacular Bronze Age barrow cemetery ❸.

PREHISTORIC SITE

The people who lived in this area, in a period from roughly 2000-500 BC, are best known for their practice of burying their dead under great circular mounds or barrows. There is a magnificent set here, some of which are simple mounds, while others are more elaborate. The path passes through the barrows and, beyond the roadway, affords a glimpse of an even older prehistoric site. The Priddy Rings  are not easy to distinguish, but they can be discerned as big, dark circles in the fields. This is a Neolithic site, constructed between 4000-2000 BC, and is comparable to the more familiar stone circles of the ancient world.

They are presumed to have religious significance, but this is uncertain.

Turning away from the prehistoric sites, the path leads back through the fields to the road down to Priddy. This is a quiet, country lane with high banks on either side. Priddy itself **E** is an attractive small

village centred on an extensive green. A sheep fair is held here every year, and the hurdles are stored in a little shelter.

Just outside the village, the route leaves the road for a walk across fields to the outskirts of the woodland above Ebbor Gorge.

NATURE RESERVE

The final section of the walk runs through the National Nature Reserve. Where the first part of the walk kept to the bottom of the Gorge, this section skirts the rim of the Gorge. Having taken the steep path down to the bottom of the valley and climbed up the other side, a signpost indicates a side turning off the route to 'Cliff Top View'. This leads out to a superb vantage point **F** on top of the limestone crags. The way then descends again and climbs back up to the car park.

◀ *At the top of North Hill there is a superb example of a 'barrow' cemetery. Bronze Age Man is renowned for burying his dead beneath these mounds.*

Underground World

Priddy is one of the centres for caving or pot-holing in the Mendips. Limestone, of which these hills are composed, is soluble in rainwater. All rain-water is acid, due to the absorption of minute traces of carbon dioxide from the atmosphere. This is a natural process, not to be confused with the acid rain of industrial pollution. Any weaknesses in the rock are attacked, so that instead of running off along the surface, drainage water runs underground. Sometimes this results from a slow dripping away through minute cracks; at other times great swallow-holes open up.

Once underground, the waters gather into rivers. They eat at the rock, creating caves, and they find new levels as they plunge down over waterfalls. The highest waterfall in Britain is, in fact, part of just such an underground system, not in the Mendips but in the similar limestone country of the Yorkshire Pennines. In places the dripping water allows calcium carbonate to come out of solution, forming icicle-like stalactites, while on the floor beneath stalagmites grow up.

Beneath the surface of the Mendips is this other world of streams and rivers, waterfalls and caves. Some of the cave systems, notably those of Cheddar and Wookey Hole, are well known and have been opened up as tourist attractions. Others can only be explored by the adventurous. Caving is now a very popular activity, but a dangerous one that requires proper equipment and expertise. It is most definitely not a case of finding a likely-looking hole in the ground and clambering down to see what can be seen. Cavers need standard safety equipment — generally wet suits with

Caving in the limestone caves under the Mendip hills. Although a challenging sport, opening up a whole new world of natural beauty, caving requires expert instruction.

safety helmets and cap lamps, ropes, rope ladders and much more. It is a group activity and no one should attempt it except in the company of at least one experienced caver.

The sport of caving offers challenges of all kinds. Some cavers are content to visit the simpler, more accessible systems; others opt for explorations that can involve anything from climbing down vertical cliffs to swimming through water-filled tunnels. For those who want to start caving, information on local clubs and societies is available from Bat Products, 8 Tucker Street, Wells (telephone (01749) 676771).

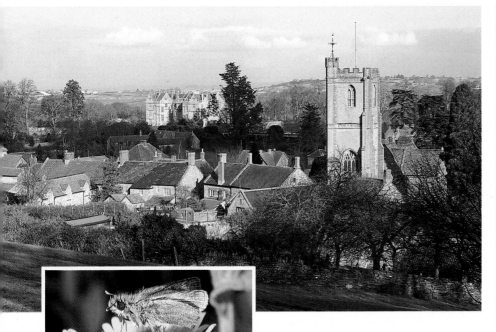

FACT FILE

⁂ Montacute, 4 miles (6 km) west of Yeovil, off the A 3088

▭ Pathfinder 1279 (ST 41/51), grid reference ST 498169

miles 0 1 2 3 4 5 6 7 8 9 10 miles
kms 0 1 2 3 4 5 6 7 8 9 10 11 12 13 14 15 kms

◑ Allow 3 hours

▭ On well maintained paths; not excessively muddy, with about 600 feet (200 metres) of ascent and descent

P The Borough at Montacute. There are also car parks on Ham Hill

🍴 The Milk House Restaurant in Montacute and at the Prince of Wales on Ham Hill

WC On Ham Hill

🏰 Montacute House, open daily except Tues, April to October

▲*The village of Montacute was the childhood home of the literary Powys brothers, whose father was the vicar. The dingy skipper (left) is said to belong to the most primitive family of butterflies.*

Through hanging woodlands to an ancient encampment

Montacute village is centred on the Norman market-place, the Borough, surrounded by Ham Hill stone cottages. On the south side of the market-place, there is an old plank door with iron strap hinges, and in the north-east corner there is a 16th-century house, called the Chantry. This was the home of Robert Sherborne, the last Prior of Montacute, and his initials are incorporated into a carved panel below the upstairs window.

Next to the Chantry is the entrance to the vast Elizabethan mansion of Montacute House. Its finest aspect is the eastern elevation, which is adorned with nine statues in shell-top niches and flanked by gazebos. This was originally the front of the house. Along the top floor is a gallery 180-feet (55-metres) long, which houses paintings from the National Gallery.

HOLY CROSS

On leaving the village, the route passes the Priory Gate House, an early 16th-century building of great architectural interest. Above the entrance there is an oriel window with a different carving under each of the lights, and right at the top there is a coat of arms carved in the central merlon of the battlements.

The route then ascends the steep wooded slope of St Michael's Hill Ⓐ, the *Mons Acutus* (it means 'steep hill' in Latin) that gave the village its name. According to legend the Holy Cross was found on the hill in the reign of King Cnut and was later taken to Waltham Abbey in Essex, which then became known as

▶ *From the gardens, the east elevation of the Elizabethan Montacute House shows its finest aspect.*

Waltham Holy Cross. The hill is surmounted by a circular stone tower built in 1760 on the site of Montacute Castle. At the top of the tower is a little room with a fireplace and four windows looking out over the countryside.

The walk continues through Hedgecock Hill Wood, where there

THE WALK

MONTACUTE – HAM HILL

The walk begins at the Borough in Montacute.

1 Turn left into Middle Street, and left again at the Kings Arms. Go through a gate, turn right, and pass the Priory Gate House. Go through a gate and along a sunken track. At the fork, bear right and cross the fence on the right by a stile. Follow the path up a valley. At the head of the valley the path turns left to a T-junction. Turn right and in a few paces go straight on, joining a well-defined path to the tower on St Michael's Hill **A**. Retrace your steps, but stay on the well-defined path when it doubles back to the left. Keep straight on until you come to a gate and stile with a National Trust sign. Go over the stile and turn left along a wooded valley.

2 At the far end of the field on the right take the stile on the right, and bear left at the first junction onto a well-worn sunken path. When you come to a stile go straight on along a little valley with woodland on both sides. Cross the fence on the right by a stile, and continue straight on. Soon the path runs along the top of the lower rampart of the hill fort **B** and there are traces of an old wall on the left.

Eventually the embankment ends and the path drops down to the left. Just past here bear right downhill. At the first junction take a path on the left which runs along the hillside. Before long the path is joined by a fence. Keep to the fence when it bends right, and turn left up a flight of stone steps. Turn right at a T-junction along a road past the Prince of Wales pub.

3 When the road bends left go straight on, following the top of the escarpment. Just before you get to the monument, bear right to an iron seat. Turn left here, and follow a horizontal path

along the side of the hill. Keep straight on until you come to a road. Turn right for a few paces (ignoring the first turning on the left) and turn left at a T-junction.

4 Take a path on the right, following the top of the rampart. After a car park, the path runs along the edge of the escarpment. Go straight on at an oblique cross-paths. When the path bends left at the corner of the hillfort take the right fork and follow it downhill through woods. Continue along a sunken path.

5 Just before a lane turn sharp left over a stile and follow a faint path up a

valley. After crossing a stile, the path passes the site of the medieval village of Witcombe **C**. From here a track goes up the right-hand side of the valley, bends right and left, and comes to a road.

6 Continue into Hollow Lane. When the road emerges from the cutting, turn right up some wooden steps and then turn left over a stile by a National Trust sign onto the Ladies Walk **D** and follow it down to the main road. Turn left into Yeovil Road, and continue along South Street to the Borough.

are badger setts, to the Iron Age hill fort **B** on Ham Hill. This is the largest hill fort (in terms of area) in Britain. Within the ramparts is a fascinating area of little hillocks, the result of centuries of quarrying. The quarries yield a beautiful, golden-brown stone called Ham Hill stone, used in Exeter Cathedral, Sherborne

◀ *The tower on top of St Michael's Hill is visible for miles around Montacute.*

Abbey and many famous houses. The area is now a country park, an ancient monument and a Site of Special Scientific Interest. From the ramparts there are splendid views to the east, north and west.

On the way back to Montacute the route passes through a deeply sunken lane where the Yeovil Sands are exposed. This rock may be identified by its distinctive outjutting calcareous (chalky or limy) bands.

A walk through the flat wetlands of the Somerset Levels

The walk begins at the village of Westonzoyland, close to the site of the Battle of Sedgemoor. In 1685, the Duke of Monmouth landed at Lyme Regis with a small army to claim the British throne. He advanced towards London, collecting supporters as he went. His bid for power ended here.

BLOODY ASSIZES

Next to the church is the Sedgemoor Inn **Ⓐ**, where an elaborate painted sign above the door tells the story of the rebellion and its aftermath. Monmouth's supporters were rounded up and tried at the infamous Bloody Assizes, presided over by Judge Jeffreys. He executed some 150 to 200 of the rebels and had hundreds of others sold into slavery in the colonies.

Immediately after the battle, 500 of the rebels were held in the church itself: five died of their wounds and 22 were subsequently hanged. Nothing in this beautiful church now serves as a reminder of those times — except, perhaps, the massive, studded main door. Inside, the principal feature is the beautifully carved roof of the nave. Although the church is a Norman foundation, most of what you see today dates from the 14th and 15th centuries.

The walk begins in the village, but soon turns off onto what was one of the main drove roads across the levels. At first the track runs

▲ *The straight drainage ditches, or rhynes, of the Somerset Levels are the home of reeds and sedges. These make the perfect habitat for the banded agrion damselfly (inset).*

between hedges and trees, then opens out into the typical wetland scenery of the region **Ⓑ**.

Left to its own devices, this area of wetland would be marshes that would regularly disappear under flood water. But the land has been steadily reclaimed since medieval times and the most obvious features are the drainage ditches that divide up the land into a neat chequer-board of square fields. They also

FACT FILE

⚹ Westonzoyland, off the M5 near Bridgwater

▭ Pathfinder 1237 (ST 23/33), grid reference ST 351347

miles 0 1 2 3 4 5 6 7 8 9 10 miles
kms 0 1 2 3 4 5 6 7 8 9 10 11 12 13 14 15 kms

🕐 2½ hours

▬ Easy walking on good paths

Ⓟ Westonzoyland village

🍴 Refreshments available at Westonzoyland, and by a short diversion at Middlezoy

THE WALK

WESTONZOYLAND – MIDDLEZOY

The walk starts on the A372 by Westonzoyland church beside the Sedgemoor Inn .

1 With your back to the church, turn left and walk down the road to the edge of the village.

2 Turn right along the wide track opposite Liney Road.

3 Follow the track until you reach the fork. A barn is set 50 yards (45 metres) back in the field to your left at this junction. Take the right fork. This brings you to typical Somerset Levels scenery **B**.

4 The track becomes a roughly surfaced road and goes slightly uphill. Where it bends sharply round to the left, a grassy track leads up to the right. Turn up the track, then immediately turn left along the path up the bank to a small gate. Go through the gate and continue straight downhill beside the fields to road. At the road turn right.

5 Where the road divides turn left towards Burrows Bridge which is signposted.

6 As the road turns sharply to the left, continue straight on along the broad track. From the path, there are views across to Burrow Mump **C**. Follow the track until you get to the gate.

7 Turn right to follow the path alongside the drainage ditch. At the broad track turn left.

8 At the road, turn right, following the sign to Westonzoyland. The road leads past the historic pumping station **D**.

9 Continue on the road as it turns to the right and follow it back to Westonzoyland, past the withy plantation **E**.

---

serve another function, acting as moats to keep the cattle that graze the meadows, so that this is a very open landscape where hedges are seldom needed.

The area may be very open, but this is a rich habitat. The ditches, or rhynes, are lined with waving lines of reeds and sedges and flashes of colour from yellow water iris and willow. In summer the meadows are a colourful sight. The rhynes themselves are home to a large population of dragonfly and water-fowl populate the wider waterways.

The geography of the area has dictated the siting of villages and farms. Where the land rises gently to a long ridge, you will see the stumpy tower of Middlezoy church.

MEADOW GRASS

As you climb up to the ridge the longer grasses of the meadows give way to a short, coarser grass. Trees thrive and the land is ploughed for crop growing. Dropping down the other side of the ridge brings a return to the wetlands and another system of rhynes. These are in general wider than those met on the first part of the walk and the pattern of artificial channels is particularly clear as they turn in perfect right angles to form field boundaries. From the footpath, there is a clear view across to the shapely hill of Burrow Mump **C**, topped by a ruined church. It is a prominent landmark, and a site of historical interest. In 878, the Danes over-whelmed the English forces, led by the Wessex king, Alfred the Great. Alfred retreated to the Somerset marshes and started the slow rebuilding of his forces. He used Burrow Mump as a look-out post to warn of Danish attack until he was ready to lead his own forces out of their retreat. By 880 he was again in control of the whole of the Kingdom

▲ *The Sedgemoor Inn in Westonzoyland — the painted sign above the door commemorates the Battle of Sedgemoor.*

of Wessex. Later the Normans came and built a castle here which was later still replaced by a church. Work was then begun on a second church in the 18th century but unfortunately it was never completed.

The path arrives at another patch of higher ground, with a farm and orchard before joining the road that runs parallel to the River Parrett. A little way further along it crosses a broad rhyne, beside which a tall brick chimney makes a prominent landmark. This belongs to Westonzoyland Pumping Station ❶.

Keeping the levels drained of water has always been a problem. In 1830, a steam engine was brought to the task, but the first version proved

▶ *A weed-covered rhyne near Middlezoy. The still water encourages algae and duck weed to flourish.*

inadequate and a new one was installed in 1861. This engine powered an enormous centrifugal pump that drained some 2,000 acres (800 hectares), lifting the water out into the rhyne so that it could eventually flow down to the River Parrett and the sea.

Today, the task is performed by a small diesel engine but the 1861 engine has been preserved in its original form and is still regularly steamed. The engine house is open to visitors on Sunday afternoons from the beginning of April to the end of October and is in steam on select days.

Once there were eight such engines in the area, but this is the last survivor. It was quite a complex site, with living quarters, a forge for on-the-spot repairs and a narrow-gauge railway for fuel supplies.

BANKS AND DITCHES

Beyond the pumping station, the road turns right, back towards Westonzoyland. An obvious and impressive feature is the high bank to the left of the road. Long before the arrival of the steam engine, the

▼ *Hawthorn in the hedgerows is rare in the Somerset Levels where the fields are bordered by drainage ditches.*

best means of controlling flood waters were such high banks, accompanied by drainage ditches. The earliest date back to medieval times and old houses have been built on top of the bank.

This country lane also supplies willows for one of the traditional

▲The ruined church on the top of Burrow Mump, the site of Alfred the Great's lookout post.

al rural industries of the Somerset levels, the growing and treating of willows for basket making. The site is marked by patches of cultivated willows ● and the simple sheds where they are treated. The obvious signs are the bundles of willows, stacked waiting for treatment or ready to be sent on their way and the boiler with its stubby brick chimney. The site can be found on the right-hand side of the road, at the point where the first of the houses appears on top of the flood bank.

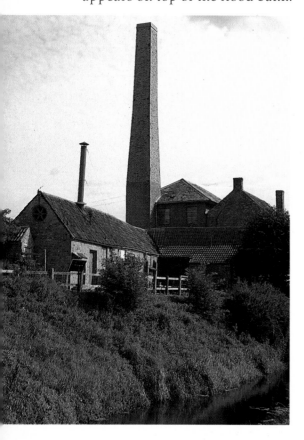

Basket Making and Withies

A characteristic feature of the rhynes that criss-cross the Somerset Levels is the willow tree whose branches hang out over the water. Some have been left to grow wild, others have been 'pollarded' — a method of producing the raw material for basket-making. The tree is allowed to grow to a substantial girth, then cut off at a height of around 6 feet (2 metres) above the ground. The new shoots, which are known as withies, or poles, are harvested while they are still slender and supple, to be used for crafts such as basket-making.

The same 'bolling', properly tended, will put out new shoots year after year. This system is used where the willows grow wild on public land, as they do beside the rhynes on the Levels.

The alternative method is to cultivate the willows as a crop in osier beds. Branches are simply stuck upright in the earth, where they root and grow as straight poles. The walk passes such a bed ●, where patches of willow can be seen at different periods of growth. Willow branches are planted and cropped every three years.

The willow is both strong and supple and it is used in three forms. White withies are stripped of their bark. Brown withies are unstripped and used to make rough baskets. And buff withies are boiled for three to five hours so the tannin from the bark colours the wood before they are stripped.

The boiler generally consists of a furnace under a simple water chest, with a tall brick chimney at the end to increase the draught to the fire. Traditionally, individual withies are pulled through a simple metal device, known as a stripping brake, but these days the stripping is mainly done by machine. The older method has, however, survived in some parts of the area.

Withy working sites are easily recognized by the distinctive boiler and the bundles of withies, which are known as bolts, either stored in sheds or standing out in the sun to dry. They are stored dry, but they have to be soaked to make them supple again before they are used to weave baskets.

Basket-making is still very much a part of the economy of the region, a genuine craft which produces objects which are at the same time both beautiful and useful.

Balloon baskets are woven locally. This one is made from cane, but many use withies from the Somerset Levels.

From here it is only a short walk to the village of Westonzoyland.

The walk has been over what some would regard as almost tame countryside, but the rhynes, the high banks and pumping station serve as a reminder that this is an area that was only conquered by man after centuries of struggle. Even now,

◄ Westonzoyland pumping station. Its new diesel engines now drain the Levels. The old ones are steamed on select days.

flooding is by no means unknown, and the efforts to prevent it, as well as to claim yet more land for agriculture, mean that it faces an uncertain future. At present, there is a balance between farmland and wetland habitats where wildlife thrive and the Somerset Levels have a unique atmosphere that many grow to love.

Through the Somerset countryside around Mells

This walk starts and finishes in the village of Mells Ⓐ. Thatched cottages, herbaceous borders, stone houses, a Tudor manor house, a 15th-century church all nestling among greens and trees make Mells one of Somerset's most beautiful and appealing villages.

The route passes the great prehistoric camps of Tedbury and Wadbury. The riverside section is a joy in spring and summer with a myriad of wild flowers and deciduous growth making it a natural park. There is a climb (not too strenuous) to the higher portion of the walk with excellent views of this typical Mendips countryside and villages.

LITTLE JACK

The Horner family have clearly played a leading role in the life of the village since the 16th century when John Horner acquired the manor house, it is said, by deceit. He was entrusted with the deeds of the house by the Abbot of Glastonbury Abbey. The deeds, the 'plum' of the rhyme, were purloined by John 'Jack' Horner. The story is almost certainly apocryphal, but is still a popular nursery rhyme.

The manor house was described in 1794 in *The Gentleman's Magazine*

as having 'Half the old house mouldering in ruins and the rest occupied by a farmer'. Since then it has been extensively restored and still retains it Elizabethan grandeur.

In St Andrew's Church there is a chapel dedicated to the Horner family. An equestrian statue by Sir Alfred Munnings is its major feature. It depicts Edward Horner who died at Cambrai in 1917.

▲ *In Mells, the village church chimes four different tunes, day and night. The male common blue butterfly (right) is blue, but the female, brown.*

Also of interest in Mells is the old village lock-up, the medieval tithe barn and the Sir Edwin Lutyens' war memorial.

During the walk the sound of lorries can be heard trundling their cargos from quarries, but essentially agriculture dominates the Mendips. The cloth trade flourished in this area from the 14th to the 19th century and made Frome prosperous. Mells Stream supplied the water for fulling (thickening the cloth by beat-

◀*In spring and summer Mells Stream has wild flowers, such as common centaury, growing beside it.*

FACT FILE

⚹ Mells, 3 miles (4.8 km) west of Frome

🗺 Pathfinder 1219 (ST 64/74), grid reference ST 730490

miles 0 1 2 3 4 5 6 7 8 9 10 miles
kms 0 1 2 3 4 5 6 7 8 9 10 11 12 13 14 15 kms

◖ Allow 2 hours

▬ One climb with some muddy patches in wet weather

🅿 In Mells

🍺 The Talbot Inn in Mells

THE WALK

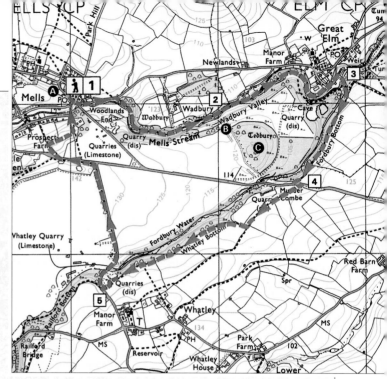

MELLS — GREAT ELM

The walk begins at the post Office in Mells **Ⓐ**.

1 ▶ Take the road going east, signposted Great Elm. After 300 yards (270 metres) go right onto an old track. You are now walking in the Wadbury Valley alongside the Mells Stream. Take the left hand path.

To your right is a disused lock and a weir. If you explore the tops of the old walls of the disused ironworks **Ⓑ**, be careful as they are slippery. As you go up the slight rise the ruins of the old iron works are on your right.

2 ▶ Continue along the track with the wooded slopes on one side and the wall on your right. Soon the stream re-appears on your right and there is a beech hedge between you and the stream.

The track leads into a lane past a house called Treetops on your left. Next take the Wyvern Way, a waterside path. After a while you come to a step stile; cross it and keep straight on. Eventually the path goes left, up and away from the stream. When you come to a stone step stile alongside a five-barred gate on the road at Great Elm, go forward straight down the hill. At the bottom of the hill the road goes right over the Mells Stream. At this point the stream widens out; weeping willows overhang it and you may see both swans and ducks.

3 ▶ Immediately over the stream turn right over a wooden step stile and left up the (overgrown) footpath under the trees. Do not take the track. At the top of the hill fork right; you are now walking along Fordbury Bottom. Shortly you go under a tunnel-like canopy of deciduous growth, which is in regular use as a bridle path. Eventually you join the main road, go left and then right and, shortly, there is a well defined track — this is Murder Combe.

Here you can take a short diversion by turning right and walking down the road to gain access to Tedbury Camp **Ⓒ**, which is on the right at the bottom of the hill.

4 ▶ The track goes alongside the edge of a field with a hedge of brambles, hazel, dog rose, sloe, on your left. The hedge peters out and becomes a barbed wire fence — keep going alongside it. When you come to the corner of the field turn right down a track between two rows of beech trees. Confronted by some barbed wire, go left over a wooden step stile into a field and make your way around the edge of the field with the fence on your right.

From this path you can see the spire of Whatley Church on the skyline. Keep going straight along the path negotiating the wooden step stiles (take care as some of these are in disrepair). On the way to the main road there are glimpses of the quarry workings through the trees.

5 ▶ Climb the broken-down stile and take care on the steps down to the road where you turn right. Walk down the hill past the quarry entrances. Just after the second entrance on the left you come to a marker post with an arrow and the word 'perimeter'. Go over the step stile and walk down by the side of the road. At the T-junction, go over the step stile and left along a broad grass track.

In a little while Mells comes into view on your right. After passing a barred gate go right over a wooden step stile onto the road. Turn right and go over a step stile on your left. Mells is below you. Aim for a sign marked footpath slightly to your right as you face Mells. Walk down to this sign and turn right, walking across the field with the hedge on your left. The hedge bears left and you follow it down to a tree in the corner of the field. Step up with the tree on your left and go right down to the stile out onto the road and back to the Post Office.

ing its fibres) and powering the heavy wooden hammers called fulling-stocks.

Another local industry was iron. Fussells established their first factory in 1744 for grinding edge tools and forging iron plates. They specialized in producing agricultural implements that were exported throughout the Empire, even winning gold medals at an exhibition in Vienna in 1860 for scythes and reaphooks. The ruins of the iron

▶ *Sluice gates on the water by the ruins of the iron works, which were once the centre of a thriving local industry.*

works **Ⓑ** are beside the stream.

The remains of the prehistoric camps of Wadbury, Tedbury **Ⓒ**, Newbury and Kingsdown are impressive and imply that this was an area of great importance in early times. Wadbury and Tedbury are adjacent to the walk, the latter being most accessible by a small detour.

The heather-covered moorland of Dunkery Beacon

This walk offers some of the best, and most contrasting, scenery on Exmoor. It starts in a deep, wooded combe and then continues to the moorland of Dunkery Beacon — the highest point on Exmoor.

The view from the car park gives a good idea of what lies ahead on the walk. The car park is at the edge of the deep valley cut by Horner Water, though the stream itself is lost from view beneath the massed trees; over to the south the view is dominated by the ridge of hills culminating in Dunkery Beacon.

TREE-CLAD VALLEY

The path leads steeply downhill through mixed woodland of oak, pine and silver birch. It slopes down to Horner Water, which winds and splashes through the narrow valley, while the trees rise up on every side, climbing the steep hillside. From the rim of the East Water Valley **A** there is a splendid view of the whole combe and the hills beyond it, and here there is the first hint of the moorland that lies ahead as heather and fern put in an appearance.

The track begins a gradual descent back to the road that now

▲ *The stony path that leads to Dunkery Beacon crosses the sparse landscape of Exmoor's high ground; the valleys are lush and green (below). The pale butterwort (inset) is found on bogs and heaths. It is covered with sticky glands that catch insects.*

runs alongside the stream. The route then leads uphill to emerge beside a beautiful example of drystone walling. Instead of the familiar higgledy-piggledy arrangement of irregular blocks, flat stones have

THE WALK

DUNKERY HILL

The walk begins at the National Trust car park at Webber's Post. It is extremely important to locate the correct path from the outset, as there are many paths and tracks in the valley.

1 With your back to the road, walk to the bottom of the car park and take the red shale path that runs right along the rim of the valley, past the edge of the woodland.

2 After the path has taken a steep dip downhill it comes out into a clearing. Turn sharp left onto the rocky path leading downhill. Continue to the bottom of the valley, ignoring turnings to the right.

3 At the bottom of the valley, turn left onto the broad track, cross the stream on the footbridge, then turn right up the footpath marked 'Stoke Pero'.

4 By a sign saying 'Nature Trail' turn left onto the narrow path

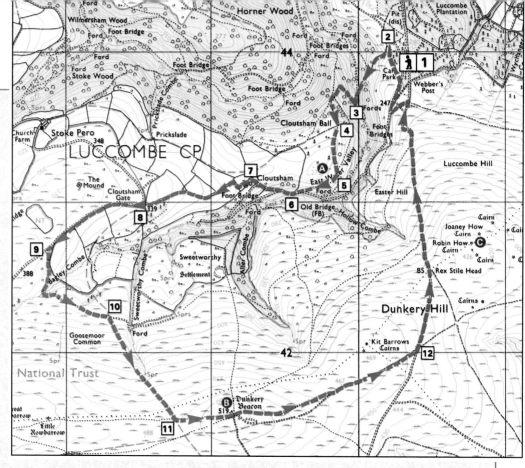

marked 'NT3' that runs along the rim of the East Water Valley **A**.

5 Where the way divides by a rough wooden seat, take the path to the right.

6 At the roadway turn right. After a little way, opposite a grassy area by the river, turn right onto a footpath on the right, marked 'Nature Trail'.

7 At the top of the hill turn left to rejoin the road. At the road turn right.

8 Where the road divides, keep straight on.

9 Turn left off the road by a sign saying 'Dicky's Path to Webber's Post'. The path goes down to the brook, then swings left to climb uphill.

10 Where the path

divides, turn right uphill, following the signpost saying 'Dunkery Beacon'.

11 At the top of the ridge turn left towards Dunkery Beacon **B** itself and continue straight on.

12 At the road there are views of Robin How and Joaney How **C**, two long barrows. Turn left to return to the car park.

▲*Exmoor ponies can be seen grazing freely on the 265 square miles (662 square km) of Exmoor.*

here been set on edge in regular courses in a chevron pattern.

Further along the route there is a change in the landscape. The woodland now gives way to green fields, where there may be deer grazing alongside the sheep. Pine and oak give way to beech. At the top of the hill is a particularly fine row of immense beech trees. It seems that when they were saplings they grew from the top of a field bank, but now the roots have grown out around the stones, so that the trees seem to stand on pedestals.

HILLTOP VIEWS

The walk now leaves the roadway for the rough path up to the top of Dunkery Beacon **B**. At first it is a stony path that leads down to a little brook, but as it climbs again it takes

on the typical character of a moorland way. It is rough and stony, and it is clear to see how it has eaten into the black peat that shows on either side. This is open heather moorland with very little shelter.

The effort of making the climb is rewarded with magnificent views from the summit. Next to the tall cairn is a metal plate, with direction lines indicating points that can be seen from the hill. On a clear day, these include the hills above Abergavenny, across the Bristol Channel, and the tors of Dartmoor.

The path continues towards the road, where yet more splendid views open up, this time taking in the coast beyond Minehead and the nearby hill, which is topped by two prominent barrows, known as Robin How and Joaney How **C**.

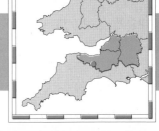
Through rolling farmland and beside a disused canal

Nynehead, a small village with a spattering of thatched cottages, is the start and finish point of this country stroll. The first part comes as something of a surprise for, instead of a conventional country lane, the road is like a miniature canyon Ⓐ, with sandstone cliffs rearing up to 20 feet (6 metres) high on either side. Overhead, branches of trees meet to form a green roof. At the top of the hill, the stone gives way to banks and hedges.

The route soon leaves the road for a farm track. Through breaks in the hedge you can see the Blackdown Hills and the tall obelisk of the Wellington monument. The distant tower of Wellington church pokes up above the trees.

CUT-SHORT CANAL

Alongside the River Tone is a trough Ⓑ constructed of thick iron plates. Once this was full of water, for it was an aqueduct built for the boats of the Grand Western Canal. The canal was begun in 1796 but never finished. Only 24 miles (39 km) were built between Taunton and Tiverton and this section was built as a tub-boat canal along which the little boats were pulled in so-called trains. For the next 2 miles (3 km) the walk follows the line of the canal

▲*The canal footpath and aqueduct (below left) are remnants of the Grand Western Canal, one of many canals planned in the 1790s, but never finished. Tall, swaying, false oat grass (inset) is a classic wayside plant of rough ground. Its flower heads resemble genuine oats.*

although it is not always obvious. The cottage by the road once stood on a canal wharf and across the road is a section of canal that still contains water; it is used as an elongated duck pond.

Beyond this is an area of crumbling masonry walls with arched

THE WALK

NYNEHEAD

The walk starts at the small green in Nynehead which has a bench and notice board.

1 From the green turn right along the road past the school. Continue straight on along the road

stile to join the narrow footpath, which passes the remains of the boat lift **C**.

5 At the edge of the field,

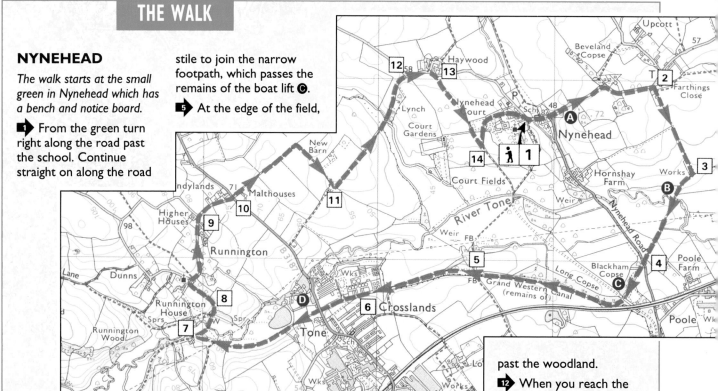

signposted to Oake, through the sandstone canyon **A**.

2 Immediately beyond Nynehead village hall, turn right onto the broad farm track. Continue straight on past the treatment works.

3 Turn right at the end of the field through the wooden gate by the public footpath sign. Follow the path along the edge of the field. Cross the bridge by the old aqueduct **B**.

4 Cross the main road by the cottage and go over the

where pathways cross by a stile, continue straight on.

6 At the treatment works, continue straight on along the surfaced road. Cross the road to the right of the bungalow and continue straight on down the path, past old industrial buildings **D**.

7 At the area of rough grassland, turn right to follow the bank of the River Tone and cross the river on the iron footbridge. Continue up to the gate opposite.

8 Follow the broad track

up to the road where you turn right, following the road around to the right.

9 At the road junction, turn right.

10 Cross the B3187 and continue straight on along the footpath by the side of the houses, and follow the path to the right as the right-hand hedge eventually turns sharply to the right.

11 At the broad, surfaced track turn right, and where that track turns right turn left beside the wire fence, keeping the fence to your left. Continue on, walking

past the woodland.

12 When you reach the roadway turn right.

13 Opposite the house called Heywood, turn right through the iron gate to follow the footpath across the field and continue on towards the woodland, keeping the wire fence to your left.

14 By the copse there are two posts with yellow-painted tops. Here the wire can be unhooked. Go through the entrance, head for the gate opposite and take the track to the left, in front of Nynehead Court. Continue round to the left to the roadway. Turn right to return to the start.

openings, the remains of a boat lift **C**. Two caissons — like very large bath tubs — were joined by chains. A boat could float into the bottom tub and water would be added to the upper caisson until it began to descend and the other to rise.

ANCIENT AQUEDUCT

Further on, there is a second, rather grand, aqueduct. The old canal is enclosed in a narrow strip of woodland, which rings with birdsong, occasionally obliterated by the

sound of a train on the nearby railway line. Where the woods end is a patch of scrubland, bright with ragwort and willowherb. Following this, a tree-shaded path leads down to the road to a complex of old industrial buildings **D** that once included a woollen mill and dye house. The tall chimney marks the days when the machines were powered by steam.

Once across the river, the route runs along quiet country lanes through the scattered hamlet of

Runnington. After a B-road, the route dives into a narrow, very overgrown footpath running between hedges. The exuberant plant life make this a little difficult for walking, but it is a wonderful habitat for insects and abounds with butterflies and dragonflies. The path comes out by market gardens and heads off towards woodland dominated by magnificent sweet chestnut trees. Finally, the route returns to the fields and past a grand house, Nynehead Court, to the village.

THE QUEST FOR CAMELOT

Magnificent views and an archaeological treasure house

▲*The view west over the ramparts of Cadbury Castle. King Arthur may well have enjoyed the sunsets from here. The yellowhammer (right), a bird of hedges and farmland, can be seen on the walk.*

The walk starts in Corton Denham, a village tucked neatly into a fold of Corton Hill and overlooking a tranquil valley almost enclosed by hills. St Andrew's Church **Ⓐ** at Corton Denham was founded in 1267, though most of what can be seen today dates only from the 19th century.

CROWDED SCHOOL

Beside the church is the former village school, built in 1845 and now used for general village activities, though its bell still hangs above the porch. In the late 19th century, an average of 90 pupils a year were taught in this one small building.

You pass a recently restored

FACT FILE

- ☀ Corton Denham, 4 miles (6.4km) north of Sherborne, off the B3145

- ⊡ Pathfinder 1260 (ST 62/72), grid reference ST 635225

  miles 0 1 2 3 4 5 6 7 8 9 10 miles
  kms 0 1 2 3 4 5 6 7 8 9 10 11 12 13 14 15 kms

- ◗ Allow 4 hours

- ◣ Some steep climbs on good paths

- Ⓟ Car park at the start

- 🏠 The Queen's Head pub, Corton Denham

horse-trough, fed by a remarkably clear spring, and wander down the main street, before making a gentle but steady climb up a track to the top of Corton Ridge **Ⓑ**.

The route follows the crest of this ridge northwards. All along here are wonderful views over the Somerset Levels to the Quantock Hills and the Severn Estuary on your left, while Cadbury Castle can be seen straight ahead as the path curves around the slopes of Parrock Hill and descends to the flat fields below.

Lanes and minor roads take you to South Cadbury, with its thatched

CORTON DENHAM – CADBURY CASTLE

The walk begins in a car park by the old village school and the church tower in Corton Denham.

1 With the church **A** on your left, go through a small, green iron gate and turn right down The Pitchen, an old cobbled track, to the road. Turn right and follow the road through the village, bearing left at a fork.

2 Turn left onto Ridge Lane, marked 'No Through Road'. This soon becomes a grassy track and climbs gently uphill. Follow it until the track divides through two gates.

3 Take the right-hand gate. Ignoring more obvious paths running downhill, turn sharp right along the crest of Corton Ridge **B**, following the line of a hedge on your right. Continue, crossing stiles,

and after ¾ mile (1.2km), the path drops a little to go through a gateway and curve right around the western flanks of Parrock Hill. Ahead is your first view of Cadbury Castle.

4 To the north of the hill, the path divides. Follow the left-hand path, going downhill.

5 At the foot of the slope, bear left through a small wooden gate to follow a narrow, tree-shaded path to a lane. Cross the lane and continue straight ahead. At a T-junction, turn right and follow the road as it bears left, ignoring Crangs Lane, into South Cadbury.

6 Go straight on to explore the village or turn left up a clearly marked track just before the church, to climb to the top of Cadbury Castle **C**. After exploring the hill fort, retrace your steps to the junction with Crangs Lane.

◄ *This sandstone church with its neat roofs and tower is St Andrew's in Corton Denham where the walk begins.*

---

houses built of honey-coloured stone. It is worth exploring if you have the time. The church, dedicated to Thomas à Becket, has a fine 14th-century tower, and an early wall painting of a bishop, possibly St Thomas, in the splay of a window in the south aisle.

The marvellous Cadbury Castle **C** covers over 18 acres (7 hectares). It is ringed by four huge banks, some of which measure over 40 feet (12m) from the bottom of the ditch to the top of the banks. Excavations begun in 1966 uncovered much of its history.

LONG HISTORY

The site was first occupied in Neolithic times, around 3000BC. Later, successive Iron Age tribes developed the hill's natural defences

into a commanding military stronghold. Within its walls grew up a thriving and sophisticated community, living in thatched round huts of timber and wattle. With trade links stretching as far as the Mediterranean, the inhabitants produced fine metalwork, some of which can be seen in the Somerset County Museum at Taunton.

VALUABLE HOARD

The Romans overcame a tribe called the 'Durotriges' here in AD70. They garrisoned the fort, using it to keep a watchful eye on the ousted community, whom they resettled below. A hoard of Roman coins was unearthed in 1922.

Excavations have also revealed new defences incorporating Roman materials and pottery dating from around AD500, as well as the foundations of a rectangular aisled hall measuring 80 feet (24m) by

7 Soon after passing Crangs Lane, cross a stile on your left by a footpath sign to Sigwells. Go through the field, to a waymark. Bear right over a wooden footbridge, then immediately left up the field. Cross a stile and continue on the green lane until you come to a gate in the hedge.

8 Go through the gate and maintain your direction to walk along the top of the field, keeping the hedge on your left. Continue on this path until the houses of Whitcombe are at right-angles to your path.

9 Take a faint path to your right towards the village. This soon becomes a track. Bear slightly left past a farm building to a gate. Go through this and cross the farmyard to a lane, following it through the village to a minor road. Turn left, then left again, climbing steeply up an unmarked road (Beacon Lane). The road bends to the right and begins to level out as it approaches the top of the hill.

10 Where the road bends back to the left, take the narrow track that doubles back on the right. After a few paces, go through a gate marked by a yellow arrow and continue with the fence on your left. Off the path and to your right is The Beacon **D**. Go through a waymarked gate and continue along the top of Corton Hill, with the fence still on your left. Eventually, the path begins to descend.

11 Where the path meets a track coming in from the left, turn sharp right downhill along a terraced path that doubles back along the lower slopes. Go through a small wooden gate and follow the path as it bears left towards the village. Turn left at the road to return to the starting point of the walk.

▲ *The view north-west from Corton Ridge, over the rich farmland of Cam Vale towards the eminence of Glastonbury Tor on the horizon. The ridge leads to South Cadbury and its compact church (below), which has a 14th-century tower.*

their spread westwards and instituting a golden age of peace that lasted some 60 years. Later, he was named as Arthur and linked with Cadbury Castle by the historian Leland, who in 1545 wrote that:

'At the very south end of the Church of South Cadbyri standith Camallate, sumtyme a famose toun or castelle... the people can telle nothing but that they have hard say that Arture much resortid to Camalat.'

Cadbury entered the history

30 feet (9m) and the outline of a cruciform church. The hill had clearly become the headquarters of a powerful Dark Age Christian chieftain and was refortified against the Saxons, who invaded Britain after the departure of the Roman legions.

Early historians recorded the existence of such a leader, who defeated the Saxons at Mount Badon, halting

▼ *From the earthworks of Cadbury Castle there is a clear view of Charwell Beacon to the south-east and of the hills that run on to Corton Denham.*

is a bench by the trig point, where you can rest and enjoy a view of the whole walk. Glastonbury Tor is prominent in the north-west, while the whole of Somerset seems to be spread at your feet.

◄*Nestling below the hills are the neatly maintained buildings of Whitcombe Farm, which has a water-mill. Further on, there is a good view (below) from The Beacon down to Corton Denham.*

books again between 1009 and 1019, during the reign of Ethelred the Unready, when it was used as an emergency administrative and commercial centre during Danish attacks. Coins were minted here.

From the castle, you retrace your steps through the village before taking a path up through gently rolling farmland to the hamlet of Whitcombe. Beyond this, you take to minor roads again for a stiff, but rewarding climb to The Beacon ❿ on top of Corton Hill. Just off the route

The Legend of Arthur

An illustration by Doré, from Alfred Lord Tennyson's Idylls of the King, depicting the sadness of King Arthur as he discovers the skeletons of his brothers and their horses.

A great wealth of legends and stories has grown up surrounding the identity of a Dark Age chieftain who flourished around AD500 and won a decisive battle against the Saxon invaders at Mount Badon.

Fragments can be found of many ancient Celtic tales about Arthur and his glittering court, but the first complete account of the legendary king is that of Geoffrey of Monmouth in his *History of Britain*, around 1135. It is, however, a jumble of fact and fiction. Arthur appears as a true medieval hero, wedded to the beautiful Guinevere and keeping at his capital, Camelot, a court of noble knights keen to undertake the most perilous of quests. Geoffrey tells of Arthur's magic sword, Excalibur, and of his last journey to the mist-shrouded Isle of Avalon – identified with present-day Glastonbury.

More legends accumulated during the Middle Ages, particularly concerning Sir Lancelot and his adulterous love for Guinevere, and medieval notions of chivalry were grafted on to these accounts.

It was Sir Thomas Malory who shaped the Arthurian legends into a satisfying whole and renewed interest in them in his book *Le Morte d'Arthur*, published by Caxton in 1485. They have never since lost their appeal, and have been retold by, among others, the poet Alfred Lord Tennyson in the *Idylls of the King* and by the 20th-century English novelist T H White in his series, *The Once and Future King*.

The search for the historical reality behind the tales has concentrated on discovering the location of Camelot. Several places have been put forward, including Winchester in Hampshire, Queen Camel in Somerset, Camelford in Cornwall and Caerleon in Monmouthshire, but recent excavations carried out at Cadbury Castle have provided evidence to make this site a clear favourite.

SOMERSET

◀ *Designed by Sir John Soane, one of the most outstanding 18th-century architects, Cricket House replaced an earlier manor house on the same site.*

FACT FILE

☀ Winsham, 4 1/2 miles (7.2km) south-east of Chard on B3162

🆗 Pathfinder 1297 (ST 20/30), grid reference ST 374063

miles 0 1 2 3 4 5 6 7 8 9 10 miles
kms 0 1 2 3 4 5 6 7 8 9 10 11 12 13 14 15 kms

◐ Allow at least 4 hours

▬ Country lanes and field paths, which may be faint. Some difficult stiles

P Beside Winsham Church

🍴 Winsham has a pub that serves food; Forde Abbey serves refreshments; Cricket St Thomas has several pubs, cafés and restaurants

WC Forde Abbey, Cricket St Thomas

🏰 Forde Abbey Gardens open daily 10am-4.30pm. Abbey open Weds, Suns and Bank Holidays, Easter-Oct, 1-4.30pm

I Cricket St Thomas Wildlife Park open daily 10am-6pm summer, 10am-5pm (dusk if earlier) winter

Beautiful gardens and exotic animals on the Dorset border

This walk takes as its base a farming village set in the gently swelling hills of a quiet corner of Somerset. From here, you walk through farmland and along narrow, grass-grown lanes, sunk between banks of ferns and wild flowers, to two stately homes. One was once a Cistercian monastery, and the other is now the centre of a wildlife park.

HANDSOME CHURCH

Winsham **Ⓐ** is a working village of solid, stone-built houses, many of which are thatched. Its beautiful hillside setting overlooks the valley of the River Axe. The manufacture of woollen cloth made the village prosperous in the 15th century. This wealth was reflected in the work that took place on the Church of St Stephen during that period, includ-

ing the tower, windows, nave roof, chancel screen and font.

The great treasure of the church predates all this, however. On the north wall of the tower is a picture of the Crucifixion, painted on wood. It once formed the back of the rood loft, and filled the top of the chancel arch. Only one other English church — that at Ludham in Norfolk — has a painting of this kind.

Among the old houses in the village is a row of cottages that are

▶ *Llamas are among the animals and birds to be seen in the Cricket St Thomas Wildlife and Leisure Park.*

▲ *The village of Winsham contains a number of charming, 18th-century cottages, many of them thatched.*

traditionally known as 'The Barracks'. These were probably occupied by men from the rebel Duke of Monmouth's peasant army. The Duke crossed the River Axe at Winsham on his way to a crushing defeat at Sedgemoor on 6 July 1685.

The route takes you across fields and down lanes to cross the Axe into Dorset. From Whatley Lane, you get a good view of the east front of Forde Abbey **B**, which looks like a Cistercian monastery

THE WALK

WINSHAM – FORDE ABBEY – CRICKET ST THOMAS

*Winsham **A** lies 2 miles (3.2km) south of the A30 between Crewkerne and Chard. The walk begins opposite the church.*

1 With the church on your left, turn left down a lane marked with a no-through-road sign. Bear right round some cottages and follow the wide grassy track. Pass the cemetery on your left, climb a stile and follow the footpath straight ahead across several stiles to the hamlet of Ammerham.

2 Turn left down the lane. After just under ½ mile (800m), you come

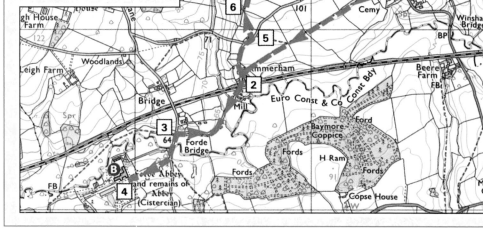

still. The chapter house, now a chapel, stands beside the long, low building that formed the monks' dormitory. Inside, though, you will discover a magnificent 17th-century country house (see box).

The award-winning gardens extend over 30 acres (12 hectares) and are charmingly informal. From the large lake that was once the monks' fishpond (now partly silted to make a bog garden), a series of lakes, bordered by rare trees, leads down to the south front of the house.

Unexpected delights await

◀ *Winsham's fine church dates largely from the 15th century although, inside, the painted Crucifixion is 13th century.*

around every corner. There is a sunken garden full of roses, and a rock garden created in an old quarry, dotted with tiny pools and miniature waterfalls. A walled vegetable garden provides food for the family and contains a nursery with rare and unusual plants for sale. The garden is particularly lovely in spring when daffodils and crocuses carpet the ground.

COUNTRY LANE

The route returns to Somerset and goes via byroads and footpaths to Colham Lane **C**. Grass grows down the middle of this neglected, rarely-used lane. Each side are banks covered with ferns and wild flowers,

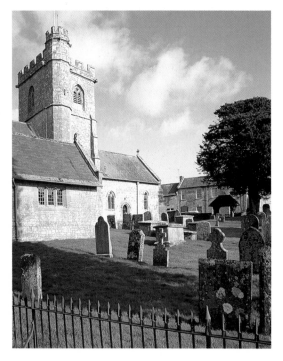

to a T-junction with Whatley Lane.

3 ▶ Turn left, cross the bridge over the River Axe and turn right to visit Forde Abbey **B**.

4 ▶ Retrace your steps to Ammerham, then go straight on along the lane. Another road joins from the left. Just past the next house on the left is a gate, on the left, with a post bearing a yellow arrow.

5 ▶ Go though the gate and keep straight ahead through another gate. Bear right, leaving some small farm buildings close on your right, to another gate. The right-of-way runs diagonally over the field to the corner. If the field is sown, walk left and right around the field edge.

6 ▶ Cross into the next field and follow the hillside ahead over fields and stiles, with a valley below you on your left. Beyond the valley, notice Leigh House, an E-shaped Elizabethan manor.

7 ▶ At a lane, turn right, then almost immediately left through a gate opposite the entrance to Hazelwood Farm. Keep straight ahead, with a hedge on your right, and continue through another gate and over a field. At a small break in the hedge, cross the wood and iron stile and turn left along Colham Lane **C**. After just over 1/2 mile (800m), you reach a T-junction with Whatley Lane. Turn left. After a short distance, you come to the entrance to Cricket St Thomas Estate.

8 ▶ Turn right down the drive, past West Port Lodge **D** on your left, and continue to Cricket House **E** and the entrance to the streamside gardens and Wildlife Park **F**.

9 ▶ Retrace your steps left into Whatley Lane, and then left again into Colham Lane.

10 ▶ When Colham Lane bears right, turn left over a cattle grid to leave your previous route. Follow a wide bridleway along a shallow valley to a junction with Limekiln Lane **G**. Turn right and follow the lane back into Winsham. Turn right down Fore Street. At the cross, turn left to return to your car.

▲ *Forde Abbey's 13th-century cloisters are a reminder of its monastic origins. Near the Abbey, the route passes the tranquil Whatley stream valley (below).*

including ragged robin, wild strawberries and foxgloves. The lane was once the only route between Winsham and the top of Windwhistle Hill. As you go along it, you are following in the footsteps of Monmouth's ragged army, walking to their doom at Sedgemoor. Progress must have been slow, as the lane is barely the width of a farm wagon.

TO THE MANOR BORN

Not far beyond the end of the lane is the entrance to the Cricket St Thomas Estate. The buildings here formed the setting for the BBC TV series *To the Manor Born*. West Port Lodge **D** was Audrey's new home after she was forced to leave the Manor; the Manor itself was Cricket House **E**. Built from golden, biscuity stone, it dates from 1786, and was designed by John Soane, one of the foremost architects of the period, for Rear Admiral Hood.

The house is privately owned, but part of the 1,000-acre (400-hectare) estate in which it stands has been opened as a Wildlife Park **F**. Parklands slope down from

▶ *The Wildlife Park houses its Asian elephants, here seen at cleaning time, in specially designed quarters intended to allow maximum freedom.*

Windwhistle Hill to a tributary of the Axe. In the early 19th century, the little stream threading the valley was dammed to make a series of lakes and cascades. The valley is now home to native wild creatures and to more exotic imports, including flamingos, wallabies, llamas and zebras, all of which can be viewed at close quarters from walks beside the lakes, or from a scenic railway.

EXOTIC ANIMALS

Asian elephants can be seen taking their daily outing, and other magnificent animals, including leopards, jaguars and several species of monkey, are kept in well-designed enclosures that allow them to live with a great deal of freedom.

There are many other attractions on offer at the Wildlife Park, and these include a Heavy Horse Centre, where magnificent shire horses are bred and cared for.

After leaving Cricket St Thomas, you return to Winsham via a bridle path and another winding byway, Limekiln Lane ⑥. This and other names — Chalkway and Chalkhill Cottages — reflect a form of cottage industry in the area. The hillside here is pitted with small quarries. Chalk was cut away and burned in kilns to form concentrated lime. This was used both as a fertilizer and in the building trade.

Forde Abbey

Forde Abbey was transformed into an elegant Italianate house, with refurbished interiors, in the 17th century.

Founded in 1180, the Abbey is a rare survival of a religious house that has been converted into an elegant stately home. After the Dissolution of the Monasteries in 1534, the Abbey church was destroyed and the monastic buildings and lands were leased by the Crown to Richard Pollard for the sum of £49 6s 6d.

In 1649, they were bought by Edmund Prideaux, who began to transform them into a palace based on Italian models. The abbot's lodging at the west end became private lodgings for the family, while the central monks' gallery became a grand saloon reached by an elegant staircase. State apartments were built over part of the cloister. The monks' chapter house, sleeping and working quarters, kitchens and refectories remain almost untouched to this day.

A tour of the house includes a visit to most major rooms. Beneath the monks' dormitory, in the vaulted undercroft, a graceful 13th-century wall painting of the Crucifixion has recently been discovered. It is one of the earliest Cistercian figure paintings in England.

Certain monks were allowed to eat meat, and dined in a separate part of the monastery from the others. Their refectory retains its original 15th-century roof, a timber, collar-beam structure, and a minstrels' gallery, below which is a screen made of Breton bedsteads! The chapel, once a Chapter House where the monks would assemble to discuss the business of the day, is a beautiful and quiet place. It has an early 12th-century vault and a fine carved screen.

The rich plasterwork of the ceilings is an impressive feature, but the greatest artistic treasures of the house are the Mortlake tapestries, specially woven for the saloon. They represent scenes from the New Testament as painted by Raphael for the Sistine Chapel in Rome. They were woven at Mortlake from the artist's original cartoons, and arrived just before a proposed visit by Queen Anne in 1714, but she died as she was on her way to see them.

THE LEVELS AND THE TOPS

▲*The village of Compton Bishop nestles in a combe between Crook Peak and Wavering Down. Wood ants' nests (inset) in King's Wood provide a good food source for woodpeckers.*

Two very different landscapes around an historic town

The western end of the Mendip Hills, beyond the Cheddar Gorge, erupts out of the flat, alluvial plain of the Somerset Levels to provide a stark contrast in land use and scenery. The lush pastures of the Levels are separated by ditches and drains, rather than hedges. This gives the impression of one great field stretching to the horizon. The hilltops are wild and unspoilt. They did not suffer from the mining for lead and coal that scarified the hills further east; apart from the occasional limestone quarry, they have been used only for rough pasture.

This walk explores both areas, and starts from the market town of Axbridge, which lies between them. Axbridge was an important town in Saxon times, and in the 11th century housed a royal mint. In the Middle

FACT FILE

- Axbridge, 10 miles (16km) north-west of Wells
- Pathfinders 1197 (ST 25/35) and 1198 (ST 45/55), grid reference ST 431545

miles 0 1 2 3 4 5 6 7 8 9 10 miles
kms 0 1 2 3 4 5 6 7 8 9 10 11 12 13 14 15 kms

- Allow 4 hours
- Some short, fairly steep ascents and descents and occasional stony, uneven sections. Riverside and woodland paths liable to be muddy. Walking boots recommended
- P Pay and display car parks in Axbridge, signposted from The Square
- T Buses from Wells and Weston-super-Mare, Tel. (01749) 673084
- Several pubs, hotels and restaurants in The Square
- King John's Hunting Lodge open daily 2-5pm, April-September

▶*The jettied King John's Hunting Lodge in The Square at Axbridge now houses the town's museum.*

THE WALK

AXBRIDGE – COMPTON BISHOP – WAVERING DOWN

The walk begins in The Square, Axbridge.

1 ▶ Walk down the High Street, between the Lamb Inn and King John's Hunting Lodge **A**. Continue on the left-hand side of the road until the pavement ends. Just beyond this, turn left down a track past Townsend Farm, and follow the lane to the Cheddar Yeo **B**.

2 ▶ Cross the concrete bridge, and turn right along the riverbank to a metal gate. Go through it, cross the stone bridge, and turn left down the opposite bank. Continue ahead across a road. At the next road, turn left then right over a stile to follow the riverbank for ¾ mile (1.2km). Cross a narrow wooden footbridge. Go half left over a little rise, and make for the stile by a water trough. Cross this and go ahead to a gate.

3 ▶ Turn left into the road, then, opposite a side-road to the left, go right up the bank along a bridleway. Soon after, the path forks.

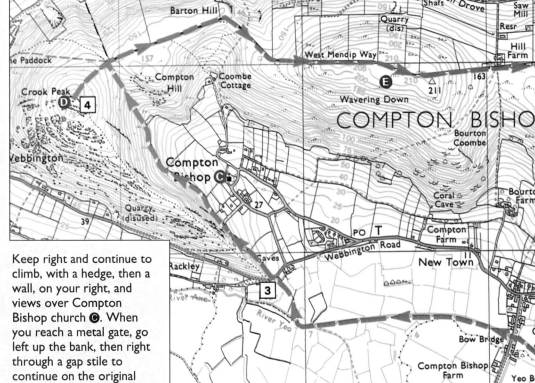

Keep right and continue to climb, with a hedge, then a wall, on your right, and views over Compton Bishop church **C**. When you reach a metal gate, go left up the bank, then right through a gap stile to continue on the original heading. Continue ahead with the wall on your right to the end of the fields, then climb a well-defined path, which narrows to a slippery channel between gorse bushes. At the top of the rise, turn left along the West Mendip Way to the rocky outcrop of Crook Peak **D**.

4 ▶ Retrace your steps and continue along the wide West Mendip Way, climbing to Wavering

Down **E**. Continue down the hill, keeping the wall to your left, past Hill Farm and on to a wood **F**. Keep on in the same direction down a broad bridleway between the trees, with the wall away to your left.

5 ▶ At the bottom of the hill, go through a car park and turn right along a road. After about 40 yards (36m), turn right down steps into woodland and

bear left. Follow a winding path into a gully. Bear right, climb the steps on the left and turn right along the grassy bank. When the path forks, keep left, on a muddy path that climbs to a busy road junction. Cross both busy roads with care, and turn right along a grassy verge on the far side. Follow this to the National Trust lay-by at Shute Shelve Hill.

Ages, it became very prosperous on the back of the wool trade, and still retains much of its medieval shape and character. It was made a conservation area in 1970.

The walk begins in The Square, a market place 1,000 years old, which boasts several pubs and hotels, and a modest 19th-century Town Hall. In one corner is the half-timbered King John's Hunting Lodge **A**, now a museum. This merchant's house postdates John by some 300 years. It got its name from the carving of a

◀ *The placid Cheddar Yeo runs arrow-straight across the Levels between pastures grazed by cattle and horses.*

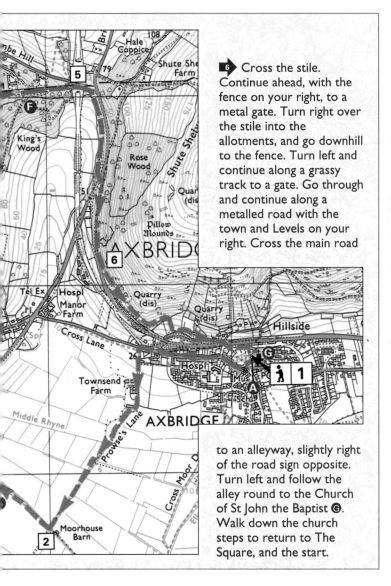

6 Cross the stile. Continue ahead, with the fence on your right, to a metal gate. Turn right over the stile into the allotments, and go downhill to the fence. Turn left and continue along a grassy track to a gate. Go through and continue along a metalled road with the town and Levels on your right. Cross the main road to an alleyway, slightly right of the road sign opposite. Turn left and follow the alley round to the Church of St John the Baptist **G**. Walk down the church steps to return to The Square, and the start.

▲ *The path to Crook Peak is bordered by a fine stone wall. The Peak's distinct outline (below, from Wavering Down) is visible for miles around.*

typical Somerset features of pinnacles and a pierced parapet (see box).

A short, stiff climb leads to the West Mendip Way and the grey limestone outcrop of Crook Peak **D**, an outstanding viewpoint. On this windy hill you can hardly hear the M5, which runs 600 feet (183m) below, through the gap between Crook Peak and Bleadon Hill.

SPLENDID VIEWS

Westwards, the Levels stretch out to meet the sea at Brean Sands and Berrow Flats. The isolated hill of Brent Knoll is to the south-west. Beyond it, across the sea, rise the Quantock Hills; Dunkery Beacon, on Exmoor, can be picked out on a clear day. Brean Down stretches across the northern end of the sands, and points towards the island of Steep

king's head on the corner — actually a pub sign from the 17th or 18th century — and from the fact that John was known to have hunted the Royal Forest of Mendip.

You leave along the High Street, past a handsomely-tiled butcher's shop. Several jettied half-timbered buildings, masked by later frontages, mingle with interesting Georgian houses along the street.

CHEDDAR YEO

The walk turns off past the aptly-named Townsend Farm to cross the Levels. The arrow-straight path, Prowse Lane, runs alongside a rhyne, as the drainage ditches that cross this low-lying land are known, to the Cheddar Yeo **B**. The Yeo and the River Axe once sprawled across this area, regularly flooding it. Works in the early 19th century straightened their courses and

integrated them into the system of ditches and rhynes.

A path along the riverbank takes you through quiet green fields to a footbridge, where you cross to begin the climb onto the Mendips. In the combe to the right nestles the peaceful farming village of Compton Bishop. You are almost on a level with the tower of the church **C**, which, while earlier and less spectacular than some, exhibits the

The Churches of Old Somerset

With the possible exception of Norfolk, no other county rivals Somerset for the architectural quality of its churches. Following the Black Death, there was a period of 150 years or so of great agricultural prosperity in this area. This fact is reflected in the way that quite modest towns and villages are endowed with magnificent buildings on a grand scale.

In common with other churches from the 14th and 15th centuries, they are in the Perpendicular style, which is characterized by the inclusion of high, vaulted ceilings, wide, tall windows, a clerestory, a large south porch and a lofty tower.

The 15th-century church at Axbridge typifies the Somerset Perpendicular style.

Towers, in particular, are a Somerset speciality. Most are at the west end, and Axbridge's central tower is unusual. The towers are divided into two, or more often three, sections by string courses, and often supported by double buttresses at the corners, while the tops are elaborated with pinnacles, pierced parapets, turrets and spirelets. Spires are rare.

The county is well endowed with building stone. Silver-grey Doulting stone is used for the churches of the Mendips, while creamy-yellow Bath stone is found in the north-east, in the part of the county now swallowed up by Avon. In the centre, round the Polden Hills, the churches are built of blue Lias, and, in the extreme south, of golden, biscuity Ham stone. All these four are limestones, and the only sandstone used is the Old Red Sandstone found in the extreme west of the old county.

▲The climb to Crook Peak is worth it for the extensive views to the south-west over the Somerset Levels to the sea.

hills, and the insects provide food for green woodpeckers, whose drumming echoes through the trees.

On the other side of the busy A38 is another woodland nature reserve, which can be visited if you are willing to scramble up the bank through the undergrowth. The walk, though, takes you alongside the A371 to the National Trust land of Shute Shelve Hill, and runs between disused stone quarries to the town of Axbridge.

You cross the bypass — which follows the course of the old railway branch-line between Axbridge and Cheddar — into a high-walled, ancient alleyway. This takes you between gardens to the parish church **G**, which is dedicated, appropriately, to John the Baptist, patron saint of clothiers. The exterior, in local grey limestone, is decorated with a profusion of pinnacles and gargoyles.

INSIDE THE CHURCH

The interior, lit by large, 15th-century windows with grisaille glass, is spacious and well cared for. There is a handsome painted plaster ceiling in the nave, and the north and south aisle chapels contain monuments from the 17th and 18th centuries, dedicated to members of the Prowse family, and showing Restoration exuberance or Classical simplicity according to date. There is also a good 15th-century brass on the north aisle wall. From the south porch, a flight of steps leads into The Square, where the walk began.

Holme in the Bristol Channel. Geologically, both of these are considered part of the Mendips.

You follow the Mendip Way east along the spine of the hills. This broad, grassy track makes for excellent walking, with good views to the right over Somerset and to the left, beyond the boundary wall, over the new county of Avon. Skylarks, linnets and meadow pipits can be heard and seen along the way.

The highest point of the walk is at Wavering Down **E**, where there are views south and east to the Poldens, Glastonbury Tor and the man-made lake of Cheddar Reservoir. From here, you descend past the isolated stone and tile buildings of Hill Farm to the edge of King's Wood **F**, designated a Site of Special Scientific Interest.

Some of this broadleaved woodland dates to before the Conquest. Small-leaved limes are found here, and great swathes of bluebells, ramsons and wood anemones appear in spring. There are many wood ant

◀The descent from Wavering Down passes Hill Farm, the only buildings on this section of the West Mendip tops

RHYNES AND VINES

SOMERSET

A walk to a winery in the gentle hills above the Somerset Levels

This walk explores a part of Somerset rarely visited by tourists — except, that is, during the long weekend of the annual Glastonbury music festival at Worthy Farm, when the area is jam-packed. At other times, Pilton, where the walk begins, is a rather secretive village. Although a main road goes through it to the north, many of the houses, built from local limestones,

▲ *Serried lines of vines spread across the lower slopes of a hillside near Wootton Winery. The greenfinch (left) has a distinctive courtship flight in spring and is common locally.*

are tucked away in a wooded hollow, almost lost among the trees.

This was originally Pool Town, an inland port that exported Mendip lead. It seems surprising now, when Pilton lies a good 20 miles (32km) from the coast, but there was a time when the village stood at the edge of a watery landscape. Up until the early Middle Ages, a vast, shallow lake lapped these hills.

OGRES AND MONSTERS

Some of the town's former importance is reflected in the parish church **Ⓐ**, dedicated to St John the Baptist. It has a tall, pinnacled tower, typical of Somerset, and a fine clerestory. Mythical beasts, ogres and monsters leer down from the walls, each different from its neighbour and beautifully carved.

A 12th-century doorway decorated with dog-tooth carving leads to

---

FACT FILE

- ✳ Pilton, 4 miles (6.4km) east of Glastonbury, on the A361

- ▱ Pathfinder 1218 (ST 44/54), grid reference ST 588408

  miles 0 1 2 3 4 5 6 7 8 9 10 miles
  kms 0 1 2 3 4 5 6 7 8 9 10 11 12 13 14 15 kms

- ◕ Allow 4 hours

- ◼ Mostly easy going on country roads and footpaths; the drove may be muddy in wet weather. One fairly steep ascent and descent. The village is possibly best avoided around the last week in June, when the Glastonbury Festival takes place at Worthy Farm

- P Limited space in the village by the church

- T Buses from Wells

- ▥ Pubs in Pilton and North Wootton

- I Wootton Vineyard is open to the public, and has wine for sale

---

THE WALK

PILTON – NORTH TOWN

The start of the walk is at Pilton's church **A**.

1 Go up the one-way street with the 'No Entry' sign, cross the main road and continue past the Pilton Stores on a road signposted to North Wootton and Wells.

2 At the road junction by the Westholme House Lodge, turn left and follow the road past the parkland **B**.

3 At the bottom of Watery Lane, cross the road and follow a rough track opposite, which leads out onto the moor **C** and bears sharp right after about ¾ mile (1.2km).

4 At a junction, turn left. As the path approaches a road, cross an iron footbridge with no handrail on your right. Turn right, back along the road. Follow this to a T-junction.

5 Turn right, and then left at the next junction, to follow a signpost to Launcherley and Wells.

6 At the next T-junction, cross the road and continue straight on up the footpath ahead.

7 Where the footpath opens out, pass through an iron gate and continue ahead for about 100 yards (90m) to a second iron gate, on your right. Go through this, and walk ahead on the right of the field up a short, steep pathway to a stile that may be hidden in the hedgerow.

8 Turn left. When the road swings sharply to your right, go through a gate on your left by a garage, and turn diagonally right across the field to a gate opposite. Continue on above the vineyard.

9 Just before the woodland, turn right through a wooden gate and go down through the vineyard to the winery **D**. Turn left onto the road. At a junction, turn right.

10 At the top of Stoodly Hill **E**, turn left at the road junction. After nearly 300 yards (270m), turn right over a stile by a footpath sign, then left at the next stile. Head towards a house with a red pantiled roof. The path passes directly beside the house. At the road turn right to return to Pilton.

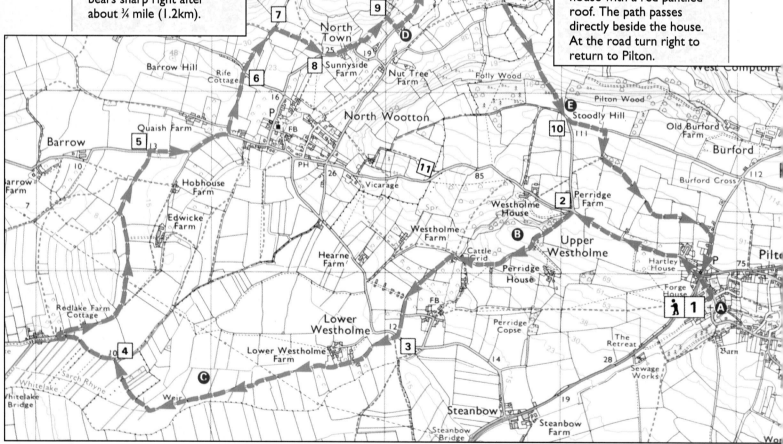

an interior that more than lives up to the exterior. Wooden angels adorn the beams of the 15th-century roof, and their stone counterparts are arrayed on the pillars of the arcade. There are some fine fragments of medieval glass in the windows either side of the altar.

The way out of the village follows a quiet country lane through flower-spangled meadows. There are wide views over green fields dotted with isolated farmsteads.

Soon, you come to the estate of Westholme House. The lodge looks rather as if it has been randomly assembled from a child's building blocks. Built in 1800, it has a wide

▲ *The stone-built Church of St John the Baptist in Pilton has an interesting series of carved grotesques.*

triangular gable end above narrow, round-headed windows, while the porch looks as if it were built for a much grander house. Westholme House itself remains hidden from view behind high walls.

At first, the lane beyond has an enclosed feel, with a wall on one side and a high bank on the other. Suddenly, it opens out to the park **B**, offering a panoramic view across Sedgemoor. The park is typical of those designed on principles made famous by Capability Brown — a wholly artificial creation contriving to appear wholly natural.

GLASTONBURY TOR

Beyond the carefully positioned trees, the flat lands of the moor stretch out to the unlikely conical hill of Glastonbury Tor, topped by a solitary tower. The road, shaded by trees, goes steadily downhill to the flat lands. At the bottom are a handsome, gabled house and a number of small orchards.

The road ahead gives way to a track, and you begin to move through a very different landscape. Beyond the farm buildings, the track becomes a green lane over the moor **C**. The reclaiming of this land from the brackish waters that covered it

began in the Middle Ages, and gathered speed in the 17th century. Rivers were straightened to speed the flow of water off the land, and a complex of drainage ditches, or rhynes, was cut. One of these is visible to the left of the route, though at first you can only see its banks, which form a hump in the fields.

ACROSS FIELDS

The new land was not suitable for building on. Droves (causeways with ditches on either side) were constructed to give farmers and their stock access to the fields. Like many of these droves, the path becomes narrower the further it penetrates into the moor. The ditches also become more obvious, surprisingly deep and carrying a very steady flow of water.

At the end of the drove, the route joins a lane leading towards North Wootton, whose pinnacled church tower becomes visible over to the right. The road begins to climb very gently towards the abrupt headland of Launcherley Hill. The surrounding fields are no longer given over entirely to grazing. In spring, the rich, red earth of the region shows through the growing crops.

The walk continues on a footpath through an avenue of trees, then turns to follow a route round the hill in an overgrown, sunken lane.

▶ *A deep drainage ditch, or rhyne, runs alongside the old drove towards North Wootton. The pinnacled tower (above) of North Wootton's church comes into view later on the route.*

▲ *Westholme Lodge, the gatehouse to Westholme House, is an intriguing mixture of architectural styles.*

◄*The unmistakeable outline of Glastonbury Tor, topped by a ruined church tower, often catches the eye. Signposts (below) are sometimes almost lost in the luxuriant vegetation.*

English Wines

Wine-making was an important aspect of life in Roman Britain, but with the end of the Roman Empire and waves of invaders from northern Europe, beer and ale became established as the national drinks. Wine-drinking never went totally out of favour — particularly in the royal households — but vineyards ceased to be a feature of the British landscape.

Since World War II, there has been a revival in English wines. There are now more than 400 vineyards, mostly in the southern counties of England. One or two measure around 200 acres (80 hectares), large even by European standards.

Generally, the soil and climate favours white wines — though there have been some valiant, and occasionally quite successful, attempts to produce good reds. The typical English wine is light and dry, and the best of them have a flowery, fruity bouquet.

The production of a good wine is dependent upon innumerable elements. The main character depends on the type of grape used, but the same vine can produce very different results according to the character of the soil, the weather, the ripeness of the fruit and other, subtler factors.

Most of the grapes grown in England are German in origin. In their native land, they produce large quantities of workhorse wines. Here, though the yield is smaller, the flavour is often more rewarding.

The Wootton Winery is one of the pioneers of English viticulture; it has been producing wine for more than 20 years, and its output is up to 50,000–70,000 bottles a year. Most wines are of a Germanic character, though they also produce some in an attractive French style.

Several different types of European grape are grown in the Wootton vineyards.

Beyond it, to the left, is a deep wooded combe. This path leads briefly back onto a road and into a lovely, narrow valley, where the first of the vineyards appears.

An altogether more open footpath provides wider views of wooded hillside patterned with neat fields and lanes, and passes above another vineyard. In winter, the vines look like lines of dead stumps in the bare soil, but in summer they come into their own, the green bunches glistening among the richer green of the leaves.

A path leads down the hill to the winery ❶, based in old farm buildings of mellow stone and rich, red pantiled roofs. It is here that the grapes are crushed and the wines fermented to make a range of dry, flowery wines (see box).

The road out of the valley is a narrow, winding lane between high banks topped by hedgerows. It dips steeply down to cross a little river at Stoodly Bridge, then climbs more steeply up Stoodly Hill.

LOOKING AHEAD

The higher the road climbs, the better the view becomes, until, at the tree-crowned top of the hill ❷, the panorama is complete. To the right is a view out across the levels to Glastonbury Tor, to the left are the low hills with the long ridge of the East Mendips behind them. Ahead is the final section of the walk across fields, with splendid views all the way to the road into Pilton.

THE BANKS OF THE BARLE

A ramble through wooded valleys and high-banked lanes

▲*Almost half of the walk is along the pleasantly wooded banks of the River Barle. The mistle thrush (inset) is one of the many birds that can be heard singing along the route.*

The southern edge of Exmoor National Park is off the beaten tourist track, but its hilly landscape, cut by steep-sided river valleys, is well worth exploring. Close to the boundary with Devon, this walk follows the wooded valley of the River Barle, then returns across high country by footpaths and lanes.

The walk starts in Dulverton Ⓐ, a little town of narrow streets and alleyways that clamber up the steep slopes to the east of the river. At its heart is a triangle of streets below the magnificent 13th-century tower of the Church of All Saints.

In the riverside car park is a bronze statue of Exmoor's literary heroine, Lorna Doone. Behind it is a building that could pass as a stately home, but was, in fact, built in 1855 as a workhouse, and is now the administrative headquarters of the Exmoor National Park.

The walk crosses the river on a medieval stone bridge, beyond which the densely wooded hillside rears up, the mass of greenery broken by the rich shades of copper beech and, in season, the brilliance of rhododendrons. For the next 2½ miles (4km), the path closely follows the windings of the River Barle. The river, though generally shallow, is fast-flowing, dashing along in little rapids and gurgling in eddies around the rocks.

The hills that rise steeply on either side are densely wooded for most of the way with broadleaved trees. In summer, they are alive with the voices of songbirds, interspersed with the occasional discordant note from a jay or a harsh quack from a mallard on the river. The gaps between the trees provide space for a rich variety of flowers.

BANKS AND DITCHES

The well maintained riverside path is never dull; at times, it runs close to the water's edge, but in other places rises and falls like a switchback, giving views down to the river. Old woodland banks and ditches appear as boundaries, and just beyond the point where the hillside has been reinforced by a stone wall, a long bank climbs the hill, with an array of mature trees growing from it. The occasional small tributary trickles its way down towards the river.

At Kennel Farm, the footpath briefly gives way to a short section of road walking, which ends near an attractive iron bridge over the river. The next section of riverside walk has features of its own: a line of crags marching up the slope, and the curiously-named Invention Wood. On the opposite bank, the scenery becomes more dramatic. Breaks in the trees near the summit of a densely wooded hill show the ramparts of an Iron Age hill fort, Mounsey Castle Ⓑ.

The route leaves the Barle and runs along a deep valley cut by a tributary stream. As it climbs steadily, there are views (often obscured by vegetation in summer) back to a grassy hill covered by a ring of trees. This marks the site of a second hill fort, Brewer's Castle Ⓒ.

BEECH HEDGES

The deep lane emerges from the woods, and the climb continues through farmland on country lanes, though the view is cut off by high beech hedgerows. The old trees

---

FACT FILE

- ⚹ Dulverton, 19 miles (28.4km) west of Taunton, on the B3222

- ▦ Pathfinder 1256 (SS 82/92), grid reference SS 912280

  miles 0 1 2 3 4 5 6 7 8 9 10 miles
  kms 0 1 2 3 4 5 6 7 8 9 10 11 12 13 14 15 kms

- ◑ Allow 3 hours

- ▬ Mostly easy going on footpaths and country lanes. Some steep ascents and descents

- Ⓟ Car park at the start

- Ⓣ Buses from Tiverton and Bampton. For details, and additional tourist information, Tel. (01884) 255827

- 🍴 There are pubs and cafés in Dulverton

were layered, so that what now appear to be many small trees are actually branches sprouting from a trunk bent level with the ground.

From the high point of the lane there are splendid views out over the hills — with their patchwork of fields and caterpillar-like hedged lanes — and back across the river valley. The land here is high and open, making an ideal hunting ground for the buzzards that soar, mewing, above the fields.

Beyond two farms, Higher and Lower Chilcott, the road gives way to a broad track. This, in turn, leads to a green, grassy lane that follows the rim of a lovely little valley. There is little indication now that its peace was once disturbed by iron-ore mining. The path dips across a stream, then climbs a deep lane to Wilway Farm. Field paths, then another narrow lane, with banks that rise above head height, lead steeply downhill back to the start in Dulverton.

▲ *A statue of Lorna Doone, the heroine of R D Blackmore's Exmoor novel.*

THE WALK

DULVERTON – HINAM CROSS

The walk begins from the riverside car park by the bridge at Dulverton **A**.

1 Cross the bridge and turn right by the footpath sign, onto the road marked as a dead end between Berry House and Rose Cottage. Follow the riverside route, which is waymarked in yellow.

2 Where the path divides, continue straight on, following the signpost to Tarr Steps. Go through Kennel Farm to a road. Turn right. Just before an iron bridge, turn left to rejoin the riverside footpath. Continue to follow the path by the river for about 1½ miles (2.4km).

3 Where the path divides opposite the high hill topped by Mounsey Castle **B**, leave the Tarr Steps path and take the left fork straight on. The path soon turns away from the river up a valley cut by a tributary stream. Continue on the path as it goes round to the left, with views back to Brewer's Castle **C**. At a metalled road, go right, uphill.

4 At a T-junction, turn right. After about 200 yards (180m), turn left onto another road.

5 At Lower Chilcott Farm, the road becomes a track, then a green lane. Where the lane arrives at two gates, take the one on your right and follow the track beside the hedgerow.

6 In the last field before the bottom of the hill, bear half-left to cross the stream at a gate. Climb the grassy slope on the other side of the valley. At Wilway Farm, continue walking straight on to the farm road.

7 Where the farm road turns sharply to the right by three gates, take the second iron gate and follow the line of the hedge, by a public footpath sign, to a road.

8 Turn left, then take the second left turning down a narrow road overhung by trees. From Rose Cottage, retrace your steps over the bridge to return to the start of the walk.

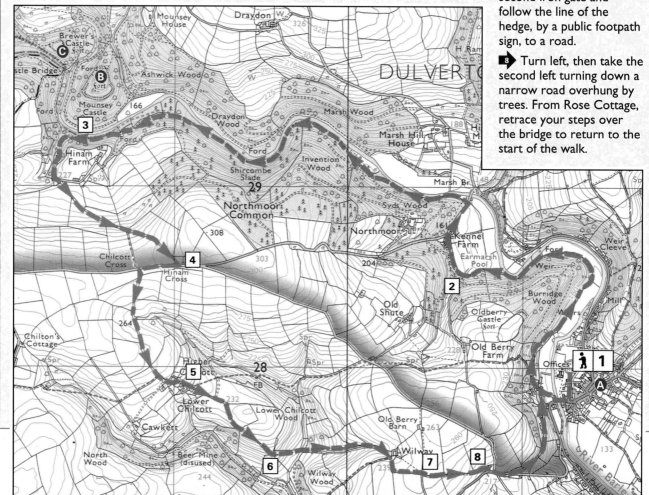

A walk up the scarp and along the spine of the Quantock Hills

The Quantocks do not cover a great deal of ground, but their woods and moors are justifiably famous walking country, offering unparalleled views west and north over rolling hills to the sea.

This walk begins below the scarp slope in the village of Crowcombe, not far from the 15th-century, red sandstone Church House. This was the medieval equivalent of a parish hall, where parties were held on feast days, and served as a lodging for travelling salesmen. In later years, it was used as a school.

SANDSTONE GARGOYLES

Next to it is a pound for stray animals, and opposite is the Church of the Holy Ghost ⓐ. This fine, 14th-century building has a tall sandstone tower, and is richly decorated with grotesque carvings. The interior more than lives up to the promise of the church's exterior.

There is a beautiful medieval font, but the chief glory of the

▲*A view down to Durborough Farm and its small fields with patches of woodland on the valley slopes. Many of the trees here are sessile oaks (left), which have acorns without stalks. The Church of the Holy Ghost (below) at Crowcombe has a red sandstone tower.*

FACT FILE

✳ Crowcombe, 12 miles (19.2km) south-east of Minehead, just off the A358

▦ Pathfinder 1236 (ST 03/13), grid reference ST 140366

miles 0 1 2 3 4 5 6 7 8 9 10 miles
kms 0 1 2 3 4 5 6 7 8 9 10 11 12 13 14 15 kms

◖ 4-5 hours

▬ One long, steep ascent and descent. Mostly good paths, likely to be muddy after rain. Walking boots recommended

Ⓟ Crowcombe village car park

Ⓣ Infrequent bus services from Taunton and Minehead

🍴 Pub and village shop at Crowcombe; pub at Triscombe

THE WALK

CROWCOMBE – AISHOLT COMMON

The walk begins in the village car park in Crowcombe.

1 Go left out of the car park, past the church **A** and along the road. Just beyond the post office, turn right on the path up the steps by a yellow arrow pointing to Crowcombe Park Gate. The route is waymarked by yellow arrows, and climbs to Crowcombe Park's woods and the old hedge bank **B**. At the end of the wood, take an obvious path up through the bracken.

2 At a broad path, turn right. At Crowcombe Lodge, the path continues past a little knoll **C**, with good views, and goes ahead to a road. Cross and continue walking straight on along the broad track to a car park area by the Triscombe Stone **D**.

3 Continue along the broad track, with the woodland on your left, for nearly 2 miles (3.2km).

4 Just before a stile and gate and beside a clump of trees, a broad track appears on your right. It turns back at an acute angle. Follow this path steeply downhill to the bottom of the valley, then round to your left.

5 At a broad track by a fenced-off wood, turn right. Where the path emerges from the wood, cross the little stream, and follow the line of the woodland on your left. The path climbs steeply uphill towards two prominent trees, and beyond them to a stile. Cross the stile and continue to follow the path up through ferns.

6 At the top of the hill, by the fence, turn right onto a broad track. At the end, follow the footpath sign to your left to cross Wills Neck **E**. Continue straight on down the very steep path to Triscombe.

7 At the road, turn right, then left past the pub and immediately right by the farm. Continue following this road, ignoring the first turning to the left by Little Quantock Farm. At the T-junction, turn left to return to the starting point.

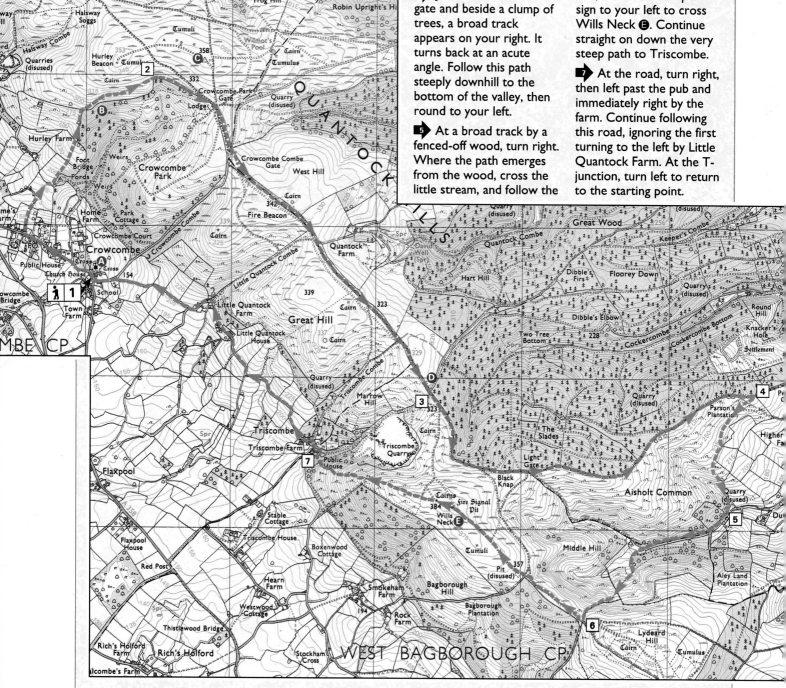

church is the 16th-century pews, richly carved with all manner of fantastic creatures and scenes, including mermaids, two men killing a dragon, and the mythical Green Man (see box on page 82).

Beside the church is Crowcombe Court, a handsome, 18th-century grand house with a pedimented facade enlivened with pilasters and a prominent Venetian window.

The village straggles out along the road. The old market cross still stands. The local inn, the Carew Arms, is named after the owners of Crowcombe Court, who also built the side chapel in the church. You pass two picturesque thatched cottages, then turn off on a footpath to the summit of the Quantocks.

SCARP SLOPE

It begins as a narrow, shady, grassy track that is overhung in places by massive oaks. There is a surprising mixture of trees on these lower slopes, varying from stately sweet chestnut to tall, spindly pine.

At first the path climbs gently, and soon opens out into grassy fields. It crosses a broad farm track and skirts a field to meet the edge of Crowcombe Park. All the time, the hillside gradually steepens; the view behind continues to improve. The valley is a patchwork of pale green fields and dark woodland. Beyond, the Brendon Hills are framed

against the rising bulk of Exmoor.

Near the top, there is a clear division in the land; one side is moorland, rough grass and bracken, the other, the woods of the park. Separating them is a high, stony earth bank **B**. It was once topped by a layered beech hedge. Over the years, what started as shrubs have become mature trees. Their gnarled roots have burst through the bank, but the trunks still show the distortions of the old process of layering.

SOMERSET RAILWAY

At the end of the woods, you enter the silence of the high heather moor, broken occasionally in summer by the distant whistle of steam trains on the West Somerset Railway. The route continues to follow the edge of the park. There are a variety of bird calls from inside the wood, but the trees are generally too densely packed for any to be seen — though a woodpecker occasionally emerges as a bright green flash as it makes a foray to the open moor.

At Crowcombe Park Gate, a small knoll **C** rising to the left of the path offers a view over to the opposite side of the Quantocks, with wide prospects of moor and woodland.

You cross a road and follow a broad track through an avenue of trees, with views opening out first to one side of the hills then to the other.

◀Near the start of the walk, out through Crowcombe, you pass the village's weatherbeaten market cross.

▲Church House in Crowcombe is a well-maintained building dating from the 1400s. Sheep (below) graze many of the Quantock fields, and buzzards may be seen soaring in the updraughts.

At Great Hill, which is smothered with mushrooms in the autumn, the route enters National Trust land.

From here, there are views across to the River Parrett as it snakes its way to the Bristol Channel, while on the other side the land drops away into the deep cleft of Triscombe Combe. Beyond that, the hillside has been stripped down to the soil and eaten away by a massive quarry.

A road appears from the left to end in a car park; close by is the Triscombe Stone **D**. This is not a particularly impressive chunk of rock, but is said to have diabolic associations. Those who come this way at night run the risk of being pursued by the Hounds of Hell.

The route runs alongside a conifer plantation. To the right, the

The Green Man

The Green Man is an image of renewal, rebirth and irrepressible life, symbolizing the union of Man and Nature.

more potent was that of the Green Man — a head crowned with flowers and leaves, with grape vines pouring from its mouth.

No one could possibly mistake the symbolism, and the Green Man can be traced back to a point long before written records. He also appears as a wood sprite, elf or fairy in a continuing tradition of folk tales.

It may seem very odd that this pagan figure should appear in a Christian church, but it remained a common motif well into the Middle Ages. At Crowcombe he can be found carved into pew ends, not once but three times.

There are a number of possible explanations. Some suggest that belief in the old Gods survived for centuries in the more remote rural regions; others that it represents a handing on of a decorative tradition that had lost its sacred meaning. The craftsmen who worked in the churches wanted to enrich them as far as they could, and were as happy to carve pagan symbols as to depict angels, demons or fantastic beasts.

A third possibility is that the carvings resulted from the Green Man being assimilated into the symbolism of medieval Christianity in much the same way as other pre-Christian festivals and totems.

warning system. The panoramic view ahead includes a great stretch of coastline, from the nuclear power stations at Hinckley Point along to the cliffs above Minehead.

THATCHED INN

The descent from Wills Neck is the steepest section of the walk, and needs to be treated with caution. At the bottom is the hamlet of Triscombe, where you will find the attractive, thatched Blue Ball Inn.

The rest of the walk back to Crowcombe is a complete contrast, a gentle stroll down country lanes, bordered by banks and hedges. Where the banks close in, you can enjoy the wayside flowers; where they open out, you can enjoy views across the farmland of the valley.

▲ *These beeches once formed a layered hedge. Their trunks were cut and then woven together parallel to the ground. There is a view over Aisholt Common (below) to the Somerset Levels.*

When Christianity came to Britain, the old pagan beliefs were banished, but were slow to die out. They survived in many customs and festivals, especially those connected with important times of the year: the death of the old year in winter, birth and renewal in the spring, haymaking in midsummer and the harvest.

Far and away the most important symbols were those connected with fertility and fecundity. One of the

land falls across Aisholt Common into a lovely, remote valley, and there is a view out to the wide expanses of the Somerset Levels. You head down, to an area of low trees and shrubs, heavy with honeysuckle and dog roses.

HIGH BEACON

A broad track takes you through the woods, with a small stream for company. At the end, an indistinct path leads steeply up to moorland on the opposite side of the valley.

Wills Neck ❺, the highest point of the Quantocks at 1260 feet (384m), was once one of the key points in the chain of hilltop beacons across southern England that served as a

THE FOVANT BADGES

FACT FILE

✳ Broad Chalke in the Ebble valley, about 10 miles (16 km) west of Salisbury

▣ Pathfinder 1262, (SU02/12), grid reference SU 040253

miles 0 1 2 3 4 5 6 7 8 9 10 miles
kms 0 1 2 3 4 5 6 7 8 9 10 11 12 13 14 15 kms

◔ Allow 3½ hours

▢ Easy with one gentle climb. Wear strong shoes with a good grip as the chalk can be slippery when wet

P Large parking area beside the church in Broad Chalke

T On bus route Salisbury–Shaftesbury. Bus stop by The Queens Head public house

▦ Refreshments available at the tearoom in Broad Chalke and
🍴 The Queens Head pub

From the Ebble Valley to the top of Fovant Down

▲ *The 12 Fovant Badges were carved out of the Wiltshire chalk downs more than 70 years ago. (inset) A guide to the badges can be found on the board.*

This is a delightfully peaceful country walk in the valley of the Ebble, a little river threading through the chalk downs west of Salisbury. An easy climb leads from Broad Chalke to a high point on the downs, giving magnificent views of another river valley, the Nadder, surrounded by curving hillsides and woodlands. Just below the crest of the down are the Fovant Badges, carved by troops stationed here during the First World War. The route follows an ancient path to Chiselbury Iron Age hill fort.

DOWN IN THE VALLEY

Broad Chalke **A** is a charming village with thatched, stone-built houses and gardens criss-crossed by the Ebble stream. The mainly 13th-century Church of All Saints has a fine 15th-century entrance arch and inside there is part of a 9th-century Saxon preaching cross. The grave of the famous designer, Cecil Beaton, is in the churchyard.

Close by is the King's Old Rectory, which was once the home of John Aubrey, author of *Brief Lives*.

He was the churchwarden, and described the church as having 'one of the tunablest ring of bells in Wiltshire'. The Rectory gardens are sometimes open to visitors on summer weekends. Refreshments can be enjoyed in the tea room (not open on Sunday mornings), which is also the village shop.

The walk takes you out of the village, along a green track for 2 miles (3.2 km) before reaching Fovant Down. Here you will come across the unique sight of the Fovant Badges **B**.

During the First World War, men of several regiments were stationed in this area and carved their badges in the chalk hillside. These include the Royal Wiltshire Yeomanry, the Wiltshire Regiment and the Australian Imperial Force. The Australian troops also carved an outline map of their homeland. A wonderful view of all the badges can be had from a viewing station in Fovant village.

▲ *The River Ebble which flows through Broad Chalke joins the River Avon near Salisbury. (left) The medieval Church of All Saints is situated by the river.*

THE WALK

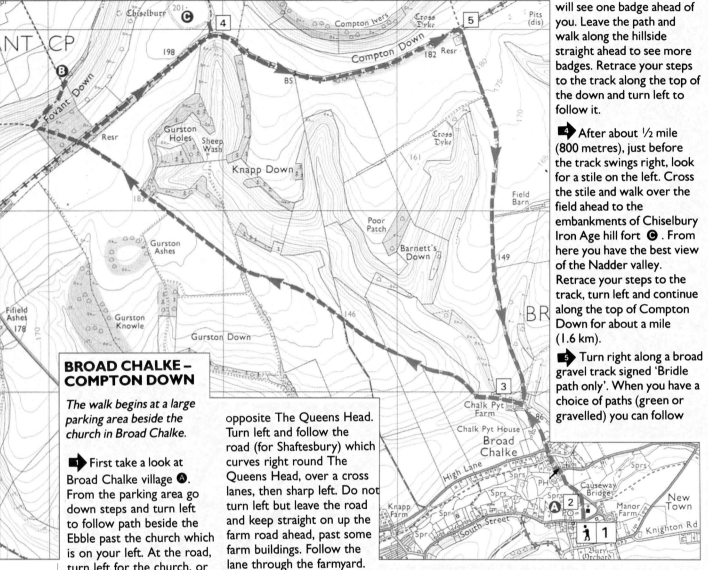

BROAD CHALKE – COMPTON DOWN

The walk begins at a large parking area beside the church in Broad Chalke.

1 First take a look at Broad Chalke village **A**. From the parking area go down steps and turn left to follow path beside the Ebble past the church which is on your left. At the road, turn left for the church, or right to see The King's Old Rectory and the village tea room. Return down path (church on right) and keep straight on past the parking area to join the road ahead.

2 Turn left, cross the bridge over the Ebble and continue to the main road, opposite The Queens Head. Turn left and follow the road (for Shaftesbury) which curves right round The Queens Head, over a cross lanes, then sharp left. Do not turn left but leave the road and keep straight on up the farm road ahead, past some farm buildings. Follow the lane through the farmyard. Do not take the bridleway straight on (which is the return route) but turn left, passing some cottages on your right.

3 Follow the green path ahead (a little overgrown at first) which climbs gently for about 2 miles (3.2km) to the top of Fovant Down. To see the Fovant Badges **B** keep straight on across the old track which follows the top of the down. Climb over a stile, and walk on through the wood ahead. When you emerge from the wood, turn right and you will see one badge ahead of you. Leave the path and walk along the hillside straight ahead to see more badges. Retrace your steps to the track along the top of the down and turn left to follow it.

4 After about ½ mile (800 metres), just before the track swings right, look for a stile on the left. Cross the stile and walk over the field ahead to the embankments of Chiselbury Iron Age hill fort **C**. From here you have the best view of the Nadder valley. Retrace your steps to the track, turn left and continue along the top of Compton Down for about a mile (1.6 km).

5 Turn right along a broad gravel track signed 'Bridle path only'. When you have a choice of paths (green or gravelled) you can follow either, but soon the green track becomes overgrown and you must follow the gravel which becomes a lane leading you back to the farm. Retrace your route back to the bus stop by The Queens Head or your car beside the church.

A short way away is the Chiselbury Hill Fort **C**. This is a very well preserved, early Iron Age fort with a single ring of embankments enclosing a large central area, capable of housing a whole village and its animals. The track leading past it along the ridge is much earlier in origin, possibly used by traders in the Bronze Age.

These chalk downs are ungrazed and, therefore, rich in flowers, including several varieties of orchids and wild clematis. Many species of birds live here, including herons which can often be seen fishing in the clear streams.

▶ *The bee-like shape of the bee orchid flower attracts bees for pollination.*

WILTSHIRE

The beginnings of modern photography in a medieval village

Lacock was home to the 'father of modern photography' — William Henry Fox Talbot. He invented the negative-positive process used in printing today, and the earliest negative in existence is the one he made of the Oriel window at Lacock Abbey.

Lacock Ⓐ is also one of the most beautifully preserved villages in England. It was named 'Lacuc' meaning 'little river' by its early Saxon settlers. To walk through this village today is to find yourself back in the Middle Ages. Most of the houses date from the 13th, 14th and 15th centuries, some half-timbered with 'wattle and daub' or brick in-filling, others built of the dove-grey local stone from the Corsham quarries and roofed in the same, creating

FACT FILE

✳ Lacock village, 3 miles (4.8 km) south of Chippenham

🖼 Pathfinder 1184 (ST 86/96), grid reference ST 917683

miles 0	1	2	3	4	5	6	7	8	9	10 miles
kms 0	1 2	3 4	5	6 7	8	9 10	11	12 13	14	15 kms

◔ Allow 1 ¹/₄ hours

▭ Level walking. Small descent of river bank three-quarters of the way round makes it unsuitable for the elderly and very young. Difficult if the river is high

Ⓟ Large, free National Trust car park just outside Lacock village

Ⓣ Buses from Chippenham, Melksham and Trowbridge on weekdays

🍴 Pubs and tearooms in Lacock

🏰 Lacock Abbey, open April—October; the house is closed on Tuesdays. There is an admission charge

▲ *Lacock Abbey by the River Avon, showing the octagonal tower which Sharington added. (inset) The pied wagtail often nests near water.*
▼ *Half of the curved supporting timber is still visible on the 14th-century Cruck House in the village.*

THE WALK

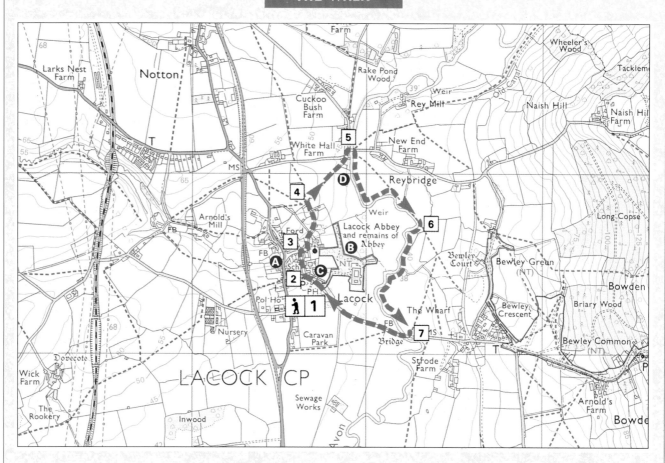

LACOCK - BOWDEN HILL

The walk begins at the large free National Trust car park just outside Lacock village.

1 From the car park, cross the road and follow the signposted footpath opposite the entrance to Lacock village **A**. Turn left when you reach the road. The Abbey **B** entrance is on your right. To the left of the Abbey gates is a 16th-century building which was originally the stables for the Abbey. Now it houses the William Henry Fox Talbot Museum **C**. Walk on towards the main street.

2 Just before you enter the wide High Street, turn right down East Street. The turning is opposite the Red Lion Inn and as you turn you will have the

Chamberlain's House on your left and the huge tithe barn and village lock-up adjoining on your right. Walk down East Street and turn right at the end with the Carpenters Arms on the corner. You will see the church of St Cyriac with its 16th-century tower ahead.

3 Just before the church turn left down a little lane. Follow the lane to cross the tiny Bide Brook by a packhorse bridge. The path runs for a little way beside the stream then meets a lane. Bear left to follow the lane as it winds gently uphill.

4 At the top of the rise, turn right through a small wooden gate and follow the path over the field (called Nethercote) towards Reybridge, a cluster of cottages ahead. You are

now in open countryside walking towards the wooded slopes of Bowden Hill. Go through another small wooden gate and follow the little lane ahead between the cottages. This brings you to a minor road.

5 Turn right, then almost immediately right again over the medieval stone bridge crossing the Avon **D** at this point (Reybridge). Leading right from the other side of the bridge you will see a wooden stile with stone steps down. Turn right over the stile and walk across the first field with the river on your right. Follow the river as it bears left. Go through a small stile near the river bank into the second field. Keep by the side of the river and where the river turns sharply to the right

go ahead to an iron gate with a stile beside it. (There is a yellow notice 'Danger - Keep Out' to the right.)

6 Cross the stile into the next field, turn right and go along the field edge with a line of trees on your right. When you get to the point where the trees end carry on to the left close to the river bank. When the field boundary is reached you will find a well-worn track leading down the river bank almost to the water's edge and up again into the next field. Follow the river to the long road bridge ahead.

7 Turn right to cross the bridge and follow the pavement back to Lacock, passing the Abbey on your right, to the car park which is on your left.

a delightfully harmonious effect.

Cruck House, with one of its cruck beams (curved roof timbers) exposed, is a rare example of the 14th-century building method. If a man could build his roof in one day, he could claim the freehold of the land on which his house stood. So two huge curved beams and plenty of thatching straw would be collected and on the appointed day all the neighbours would be called in to help erect the roof.

▲ *The 'lock-up' where the drunk and disorderly were kept overnight.*
◀ *The Lacock church is dedicated to the child martyr, St Cyriac.*

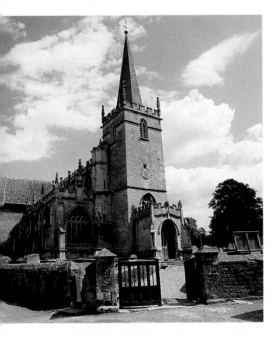

A massive tithe barn with eight large bays is a reminder of the time when the villagers had to pay their rent in produce to the Abbey. Later the barn became the market hall as Lacock flourished with the growth of the wool trade. The wealth of the inhabitants, based on spinning and weaving, is reflected in the quality of their well-built homes, all pleasing to the eye and no two exactly alike. Among the few 18th-century buildings is a small domed 'lock-up'. Within living memory, the sympathetic villagers would refresh the unfortunate imprisoned victims with saucers of tea — cups were too large to go under the door!

PRESERVATION OF LACOCK

The Talbot family who owned Lacock transferred it, with the Abbey, to the National Trust in 1944. The Trust has conserved it wisely, as exemplified by their solution to the problem of television reception. In the village there is not an aerial in sight — television is piped into Lacock from a single aerial on a nearby hillside.

As you look through the gates from the village across the wide lawns that sweep down to the River Avon you can see the elegant 18th-century west front of Lacock Abbey **B**. Inside, many of the features of the 13th-century religious house have been preserved. Lacock Abbey was founded by Ela, Countess of Salisbury in 1232 for Augustinian nuns. The sacristy, the chapter house and the warming room date from her time. Lacock Abbey was the last religious house in England to be closed during the Dissolution, as Henry VIII's commissioners could find no fault with the nuns who were 'of virtuous living'.

CONVERTING THE ABBEY

In 1540 the Abbey was bought by Sir William Sharington who kept much of Ela's original building and the beautiful cloisters, which had been rebuilt in the 15th-century. He converted these medieval features into his own dwelling house, adding console windows and Tudor chimneys to the refectory and dormitory, and built a fine octagonal tower in the south-east corner.

It was through the marriage of his niece Olive that the Abbey passed to the Talbot family. Olive was refused permission to marry a Talbot and locked in her room, but in defiance, she leapt from her window into the arms of her lover. Impressed by her bravery, the Sharingtons relented and the couple were married

In 1754, John Ivory Talbot employed Sanderson Miller to design a new Hall for the Abbey. It is decorated with terracotta figures

▼ *The water meadows beside the River Avon near Lacock Abbey.*

Pioneer of Photography

The earliest negative (far right) shows the Oriel window (above) at Lacock Abbey from the inside.

William Henry Fox Talbot pioneered the negative-positive technique of printing photographs that is used today.

Fox Talbot was born on 11th February 1800. When his father died, leaving heavy debts, his mother leased out the Lacock estate to raise money. The family returned to live at Lacock Abbey 27 years later.

As a student, Fox Talbot proved equally brilliant at the arts and sciences. When on honeymoon in Italy with his wife Constance, he grew impatient with his sketching, wishing 'to cause these natural images to imprint themselves durably and remain fixed on paper'. His scientific experiments to achieve this began on his return home.

His first task was to find a light-sensitive coating for paper that made the paper go dark in areas exposed to light. Later he found a way of using these 'negatives' to produce a print 'in which the light and shadows would be reversed'. He called these photographs 'photogenic drawings'.

By 1840, Fox Talbot was producing what he called 'calotype' photographs, using improved lenses and more sensitive bromide paper. With the reduction of exposure time, he was able to take portraits.

In 1844-6, Longman's published his book called *The Pencil of Nature*. It was the first book to be illustrated with real photographs. Fox Talbot died in 1877, content in the knowledge that his achievements in photography would inspire others.

in niches and Talbot must have pleased his friends, the local landowners, when he had the Hall ceiling painted with their coats of arms. The Abbey remains a family home, for descendants of the Talbots still live there as tenants of the National Trust.

A 16th-century barn near the approach to Lacock Abbey has been converted into the William Henry

The packhorse bridge over Bide Brook, the 'little river' to which 'Lacock' refers.

Fox Talbot Museum **C**. Opened in 1975, it houses a collection of historic photographs and photographic equipment as well as material relating to the life and scientific research of Fox Talbot.

The River Avon **D** curves around the grounds of the Abbey. It was important to the medieval settle-

The Warming Room at the Abbey with the nuns' cauldron on display.

ment of Lacock as a trade route to and from the port of Avonmouth. Today, walking by the river, you can watch the ducks and moorhens swimming by the reeds, and herons fishing in the shallows.

The Wylye Valley

From streamside paths to downland views and dense woodland

This walk starts close to Steeple Langford, a lovely village beside the River Wylye, which meanders through the widest of the river valleys west of Salisbury. The attraction of this walk is its variety. From the village, little paths follow the banks of the stream through water meadows. A gentle climb on to the downs is rewarded by magnificent views from the embankments of an Iron Age fort. And the

route includes a woodland stroll along the line of a Roman road.

The River Wylye flows through Steeple Langford Ⓐ and several of the houses have lawns sweeping down to the water. Some of the houses in the village are built in the distinctive chequer designs found in areas of chalk and flint. The parish Church of All Saints has a rare 12th-century Purbeck marble font and a Saxon cross circa 850 AD.

Close to the village, the Wylye divides into several small streams overhung with willows and bordered by flowers. Narrow paths follow the streams, crossing over wooden bridges, making delightful

▲ *The river Wylye makes a good setting for houses in Steeple Langford (left). The silver-washed fritillary (inset) is a woodland butterfly.*

walks. Seats beside the streams are ideal places for picnics. These small streams probably gave Steeple Langford its name. 'Steeple' may derive from the staples or posts marking the line for crossing the long ford, which was more than 1/4 mile (400 metres) across the River Wylye at this point. It is also possible that 'staple' indicated that the area had a market.

At the top of the downs overlooking the Wylye Valley is Hanging Langford fort Ⓑ. The embankments of this Iron Age fort are well preserved. The area covered is so extensive that the fort could have served to protect a whole village

FACT FILE

- ✳ Steeple Langford in the Wylye valley, 8 miles (12.8 km) north-west of Salisbury

- 🚌 Pathfinder 1241 (SU 03/13), grid reference SU 036368

  miles 0 1 2 3 4 5 6 7 8 9 10 miles
  kms 0 1 2 3 4 5 6 7 8 9 10 11 12 13 14 15 kms

- ◔ Allow 3 1/2 hours

- ▬ Easy with a short gentle climb. Strong shoes recommended

- P Parking area on right down Duck Street, between Steeple Langford and Hanging Langford

- T On the bus route from Bristol to Salisbury via Bath

- 🍴 Pub and shop in Steeple Langford

THE WALK

STEEPLE LANGFORD – GROVELY WOOD

Drive into Steeple Langford **A** *in the direction of the church, and turn down Duck Street, a minor road leading to Hanging Langford. After 1/4 mile (400 metres) there is a T-junction sign and just before it, a parking area on the right where the walk begins.*

▶ **1** From the parking area, walk up the lane to the T-junction. Turn right for a short distance, then take the first lane on your left, by a sign 'Harroway'. Go under the railway and through a wooden gate and follow the path as it climbs

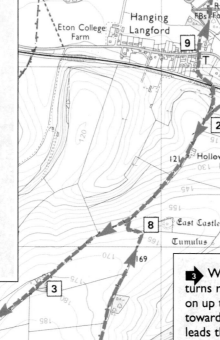

▶ **3** When the chalk track turns right, keep straight on up the green path ahead towards a wood. The path leads through the wood to the open grassy top of the Downs. Follow the main path over all crosstracks. After crossing a stile, cross the embankments of Hanging Langford hillfort **B**. From here there are marvellous views across the beautiful Wylye Valley.

▶ **4** When you come to a gate, go through and keep on till you come to a crosstrack – the Roman road **C**. Turn left along the Roman road (metalled but clearly defined and embanked).

▶ **5** A large barn appears directly ahead with paths to right and left. Follow the right-hand path (still the Roman road) past Forestry Commission sign into Grovely Wood **D**.

▶ **6** After about 3/4 mile (1200 metres) look carefully for a crosstrack with a post on the left marked with white arrows. Turn left and follow the path through the wood until you come to a crossing path on the edge of the wood. Turn left and walk for about 50 yards (45 metres).

▶ **7** Turn right down the first track on the right (marked by a white arrow on a post). Continue downhill with the hedge on your right.

▶ **8** At the crosstrack turn left to rejoin the earlier path. This time, ignore the small wooden gate on your right and continue downhill to the minor road at Hanging Langford.

▶ **9** Cross straight over the road and follow the little path ahead that winds beside the Wylye, over two bridges to Steeple Langford church. Turn right to walk across the churchyard and through the lych gate to Duck Street. Turn right to walk back to your car or left to bus stop.

through trees to a second small wooden gate. (The path is cleared regularly but may be a little overgrown for only a short distance.)

▶ **2** Go through the gate and continue uphill on the chalk track to the right of the gate. Keep straight on past a joining track on your left.

▲ *A traditional cottage near Hanging Lanford chequered in flint and stone.*

and outlying homesteads.

After the hillfort, the walk enters Grovely Wood **D** along the Roman road **C**. This has been roughly met-alled, but it is possible to see the embankments. The road probably connected Bath and Salisbury.

Grovely Wood is a large area of woodland that now belongs to the Forestry Commisssion. By ancient right, the villagers of Great Wishford, 3 miles (4.8 km) east of Steeple Langford, can gather wood there. An Oak Apple Day ceremony is held annually on 29th May in celebration of this custom.

▼ *Much of the downland above the Wylye Valley is farmed.*

WILTSHIRE

A walk along a Roman road high above the Calne Valley

Calstone Wellington is a tiny, isolated village beside a wooded valley, sheltered by the north-western rim of the Marlborough Downs. It is part of the Bowood Estate, the family home of the Marquess of Lansdowne. The Georgian Bowood house can be seen on the opposite hillside, 2 miles (3.2 km) west of Calne.

The village must once have been much more extensive than it is now and its position points to a fascinating history. Some distance from any through routes, the original settlement was made on the 'spring line'. (Springs occur when the water seeping down through the chalk layer meets a harder substance, usually on the lower slopes.) The little River Marden rises out of the down at Calstone to provide the villagers with their water today, just as it did when the first farmers settled here in prehistoric times.

In the churchyard, the discovery of a Bronze Age brooch, decorated with spirals, is evidence of the area's long habitation. Early Iron Age field

▲ *The Bridleway leads to the Roman Road where the surrounding downs are designated as a Nature Reserve. This area provides sanctuary for badgers (right) and other wildlife.*

FACT FILE

✳	Calstone Wellington, a small village 3 miles (4.8 km) south-east of Calne
▭	Pathfinder 1185 (SU 06/16), grid reference SU 020686

miles 0 1 2 3 4 5 6 7 8 9 10 miles
kms 0 1 2 3 4 5 6 7 8 9 10 11 12 13 14 15 kms

🕐	Allow 3 hours
▬	Exposed, but generally easy
P	Large parking area immediately before the Calstone village sign
🍴	Hotels and restaurants 1 mile (1.6 km) away at Hayle Farm and along the road to Cherhill
🏠	The Black Horse in Cherhill

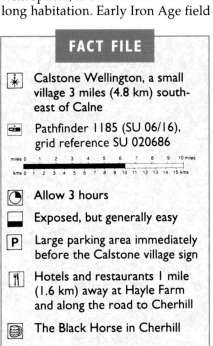

systems terrace nearby Cherhill Down and later Celtic peoples, coming under Roman influence, must also have lived here. Romano-British pottery has been found in the valley, just south of Manor Farm.

On the down above Calstone Wellington lies the beautifully cared-for St Mary's Church Ⓐ, and

this is well worth a visit. In the south window of the chancel, there is a panel containing fragments of medieval glass, glowing with colour. The walls of the church are covered with old graffiti, with some of the dates and initials carved in the stone

THE WALK

CALSTONE WELLINGTON

The walk begins at the large parking area in Calstone Wellington. Take the A361 from Devizes and turn left along a minor road for Calne after about 4 miles (6 km). After a little over 3 miles (5 km), look carefully on your right for the turning for Calstone. Park in the large parking area to the left of the road immediately in front of the Calstone village sign.

1 With the village sign on your left, walk up the lane past the turning for Compton Bassett. Keep on through the village, past Manor Farm and the Manor. The road dips to cross a little valley with a small lake on the right and then divides. Turn right up the lane following the sign to St Mary's Church **A** and The Old Rectory.

2 Just before St Mary's Church you will see an iron gate on your right. Go through the gate, turn left and walk up the field with the church tower and fence on your left. Where the fence ends, keep straight on to a gate on your left. Go through the gate, turn right and follow the hedge to a gate leading to a bridleway. Turn left and follow the bridleway for about 50 yards (46 metres). Now turn right and follow the bridleway that lies ahead.

3 The path dips and you will see a gate on your left. Turn left through the gate, then bear right to a terraced green path you will see ahead, bearing left along the hillside. The path bears round to the right, with a small valley leading to a wooded hillside on your left. Sweeping downland views begin to open around you. Go through the next gate and keep straight on uphill. After the next gate walk a few yards to your right to follow the fence uphill in the same direction. There are several prominent round Bronze Age burial mounds, or barrows **B**, on your left. Ahead of you is a small wooden gate.

4 Go through the gate. Immediately on your left you will see the Roman Road **C**, now a superb green track. Meeting the road at this point you will see the Wansdyke **D**, also leading left. Turn left along the Roman Road, past the sign indicating the area to be a Nature Reserve. Now follow the wide path along the course of the Roman Road for about 2 miles (3 km). There are marvellous views of the Calne valley.

5 Just past a narrow belt of trees on your right you come to a crosstrack. Turn left through a gate and walk straight ahead uphill with a fence on your right.

Crowning the hill ahead you will see Oldbury Camp **E**. As you near the top, the path dips between the embankments that protected the southern entrance to the fort. Keep straight on through a gate, past a National Trust sign, to the top of the hill with the circular embankments of the fort on your left.

6 When you meet a gravel track turn left and, when the gravel ceases, keep straight on towards the tall Cherhill Monument **F** that you see ahead.

7 Walk around the monument along the crest of the down. After about 50 yards (46 metres) look to your right at the sloping hillside and you will see part of a white horse **G** carved out of the turf. Return to the monument, but just before you reach it, you will see a stile on your right. Cross this and then bear right along the green descending track you will see ahead. When the path divides, bear left towards a fence. The path curves around to the right to bring you to the crest of the down again. Look right here for a splendid view of the white horse.

8 Do not go downhill, but bear left towards a small clump of trees (damaged by storms). Keeping the trees close on your right, walk past a

hollow on your left. There is no clear path for the next 100 yards (91 metres) so be very careful here. When the woods end, do not follow the narrow paths bearing left over the down, but keep on over the down, bearing a little right and downhill. You quickly come to an excellent, well-marked path. Follow this down to a stile. Cross the stile and follow the path ahead that runs along the valley between high banks.

9 Just in front of two large barns, a track joins from the right. Turn left here through a gate and follow the path straight ahead with a fence close on your right, in the direction of two large aerials on the down ahead. Go through a gate and keep on with the fence on your right.

10 After the next gate, walk straight on for about 50 yards (46 metres) and look for a small iron gate on your left. Go through and follow the little path through woods down into a little valley. Bear right over a bridge that crosses a small stream flowing into a lake and follow the lane uphill back to Calstone Wellington. When you meet a minor road, turn right and continue past a farm and through the gates to return to the car park at the start of the walk.

◀ *A story-book thatched cottage in the village of Calstone Wellington typifies traditional West Country architecture.*

dating back to the early-17th century. The north porch is quite large, with stone benches at either side and a tiny round window. It is said to have been used in the past as the local lock-up in the absence of a gaol.

This area of the Marlborough Downs is dotted with round Bronze Age burial mounds or barrows **B**. Invaders with knowledge of bronze smelting reached this area around 1800 BC. A wealthy society developed as trade in salt, bronze, Baltic amber, Irish gold and Whitby jet flourished along the trackways.

The burial mounds vary a little in their construction as you will see — they can be bell-, bowl- or disc-

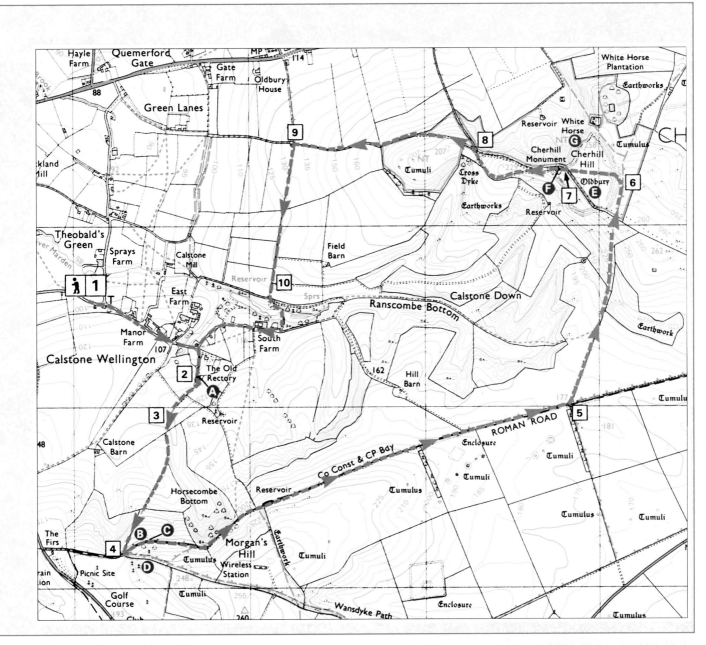

shaped. Bodies were sometimes cremated and buried with grave-goods, including finely worked bronze and gold daggers and bracelets and necklaces of blue faience beads from Egypt. Collections of these grave-goods can be seen in Devizes museum.

ROMAN ROAD

Running west from the Thames Valley to Bath, the splendid embanked Roman road ● is the equivalent of today's A4. You can clearly see the construction method employed. The road had to be wide (ten legionaries had to be able to march abreast), embanked and, in this case, terraced along the side of

the down. The surface had to be hard and flat for quick and easy marching and the passage of chariots and waggons. Having made the terrace, surplus earth was heaped along the centre; large heavy stones were laid over this and these, in turn, were topped with a rammed

◄ *St Mary's Church is on the down above Calstone Wellington. The south window of the chancel (above).*

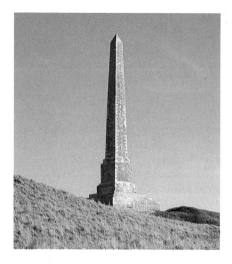

▲ *The Cherhill Monument is 125 ft (7.5 metres) high; it was erected in the 19th century in memory of Sir William Petty.*

layer of crushed stones and flints.

The fenced, ungrazed margins of the road are exceptionally rich in wild plants. Among them you could possibly see pink and white wild candytuft, yellow sprays of ladies' bedstraw, tall blue clustered bell-flowers and pyramidal and bee orchids. The Roman road and the surrounding downs are designated as a Nature Reserve. Animals include foxes, badgers and hares. Kestrels and buzzards hover over-head. Butterflies include chalkhill blues, dark green frittillaries and the lovely marbled white.

IRON-AGE HILLFORT

Intersecting with the Roman road, the great ditch of the Wansdyke ⓓ was probably dug by Celtic tribes during the Iron Age to mark their territorial boundaries. Later, Christianised peoples called the

White Horses

Wherever chalk downlands raise their curved outline against the sky, you will find hill figures. The thin layer of turf can be removed easily, then pounded chalk pressed firmly in and levelled. The most popular hill figure is a horse.

The greatest concentration of white horses is to be found on the chalk hill slopes of Wessex. The Uffington White Horse is the oldest and certainly the most beautiful. Its graceful outline appears to float across the Oxfordshire downs beneath the ramparts of the Iron Age hillfort. Its origins are still uncertain, but it is probable that it was carved by the Belgae, a late Iron Age people.

The oldest white horse in Wiltshire is high on the downs above Westbury. King Alfred is said to have ordered it to commemorate his victory over the Danes in the 9th century. Originally a stocky hill pony such as Alfred would have used for his cavalry, it was 'improved' by a Mr Gee in 1778. This inspired many imitations.

Sometimes royal occasions led to the creation of white horses. The Hackpen horse near Winterbourne Bassett in Wiltshire is said to have been cut to commemorate the

coronation of Queen Victoria, while the figure of George III on horseback near Osmington commemorates the visits that this monarch made to Weymouth in order to improve his health and review his army.

Some horses, however, appear to have been carved just for fun! The famous Yorkshire white horse on Roulston Scar above Kilburn was carved out of the turf in 1857 by the local schoolmaster, Thomas Hodgson, ably assisted by the boys of the village.

The oldest known White Horse in Wiltshire is the Westbury Horse on Bratton Down, originally dating from the 9th century.

ditch 'Woden's Dyke', believing it to be the work of the devil.

Commanding the crest of Oldbury Hill, the Iron Age hillfort of Oldbury Camp ⓔ encloses 25 acres (10 hectares) of land and is defended by double banks and ditches. The Iron Age tribes constructed these forts to defend their settlements. They were fine warriors and expert sling shots, but no match for the Roman legions who set about con-quering Wessex after the Claudian invasion in AD 45.

Shortly after Oldbury Camp, you arrive at the Cherhill Monument ⓕ. The third Marquess of Lansdowne erected this column to commemo-rate one of his ancestors, Sir William Petty, a 17th-century economist.

◀ *The Roman Road on the walk was once part of a direct route from Bath, across the downs, to the Thames Valley.*

Looking out to the right of the Monument, you will see the white horse ⓖ, carved out of the turf on the steep hillside where it falls away beneath the hillfort ramparts.

CUTTING THE HORSE

It was cut in 1780 when landowners were perhaps inspired by new interest in the historic white horse on the Oxfordshire downs near Uffington. Its creator was Dr Christopher Alsop, of Calne. Dr Alsop is said to have shouted his instructions through a megaphone from the middle of Cherhill village to the workmen on the down, who then planted white flags to mark the outline. The result is a well-propor-tioned animal, 140 feet (43 metres) long. Originally, the horse's eye was set with bottles, which must have sparkled attractively in the sunlight, but these have disappeared.

OLD SARUM

Old Sarum became one of the 'rotten boroughs' of the 18th century, returning two MPs from an electorate of 10 people. One of them was William Pitt the Elder.

The surrounding downs were once covered with beech woods — until ancient man began felling them. Though the downs are mostly grassland now, the beech is still the most common tree. The grasslands support a wide range of flowering

◀ *The castle of Old Sarum and the remains of the cathedral all surrounded by the defensive earthworks that protected the old city. Mayfly (inset) can be found along the River Avon.*

FACT FILE

* Old Sarum, 2 miles (3.2 km) north of Salisbury on the A345, Wiltshire

* Pathfinder 1241 (SU 03/13), grid reference SU 139326

| miles 0 | 1 | 2 | 3 | 4 | 5 | 6 | 7 | 8 | 9 | 10 miles |
| kms 0 | 1 2 3 4 5 6 7 | | 8 | 9 10 11 12 13 14 15 | kms | | | | | |

* Allow 2¼ hours

* Easy, well marked footpaths and bridlepaths. Good walking shoes recommended, some muddy patches in winter

* P Old Sarum car park

* WC Toilets in car park, pub in Stratford sub Castle and opposite Old Sarum across main road

A walk around an ancient fortress and along the Avon

hectares) and impart a strong sense of vanished glory. The remains of the Norman keep are today neatly labelled by the owners, English Heritage. From the castle walls the foundations of the Norman cathedral can be seen. William the Conqueror had paid off and demobilized his victorious army here and his nephew Bishop Osmund completed the first cathedral.

In 1220, Bishop Herbert Poore decided to move from Old Sarum. His clergy had been locked out of the city after returning from a procession and this was the final straw in a long-running dispute. Old Sarum already had a shortage of water and now stands deserted while its thriving successor, Salisbury, flourishes below.

O nce a fortress of the Ancient Britons, the Romans called it Sorviodunum, the Saxons Searisbyng and the Normans Sarisberie. But a bitter feud between the clergy and the military at the beginning of the 13th century proved a decisive turning point in the history of this ancient place.

Sited on a hill-top, the multiple earthworks **A** cover 56 acres (23

▶ *Little Durnford Manor Estate can be seen best from the other side of the Avon. Flint is a popular building material in the area.*

THE WALK

OLD SARUM – LITTLE DURNFORD

The walk begins from the car park in Old Sarum.

▶ From the car park walk back towards the A345 and turn sharp left over a new step stile up a track 30 yards (27 metres) before you reach the road. You walk around the north-eastern side of Old Sarum with the earthworks **A** on your left. At the road, climb over a new padlocked gate. Turn right. Walk 50 yards (45 metres) down the road, then left down the signposted bridle-path. Just past Shepherds Corner the track climbs the downs past a rectangular-shaped coniferous plantation on your left **B**. The climb starts to ease with open fields to left and right. Keep straight on as the track descends, with new planting on the right, to a white, thatched Keeper's Cottage with a satellite dish.

▶ Turn left immediately before the cottage and continue down the metal track of the avenue. Cross the road and go through the white gate marked 'footpath'. Walk through the grounds of Little Durnford Manor. At a junction take the right-hand fork which takes you past the stables on your left to the bridge over the Avon. Cross the bridge and walk through the water meadow and up to the road.

▶ At the road turn left where it is signposted to Salisbury. (Look left for your best view of the Durnford Manor Estate.) Turn right immediately after Avon Farm Cottage, through a white metal gate. Pass Avon Farm House on your left. Go through a gate and along the side of the field with a hedge on your left. The hedge gives way to a wooden post and wire fence before you reach the adjacent corner of the field. Leave by a wooden step stile. After some 22 yards (20 metres), another wooden step stile brings you onto a path bordering a meadow. Follow the path as it goes between a hedge to your right and a stand of young beech trees to your left, climbing slightly above the meadow. The River Avon then runs close to your path. You can see the irrigation ditches which were dug herringbone-style in the meadow below and to your left. After crossing another step stile, the River Avon is almost immediately below on your left.

▶ On arriving at a junction with a metalled path, turn left and cross the bridge over the River Avon **C**. Go right at the road into the village of Stratford sub Castle. Immediately after the thatched Old Forge Cottage cross the road and turn left following a path signposted 'Old Sarum'. At the top of the path go right over a wooden stile and around the bottom of Old Sarum to return to the beginning of the walk.

◀ *The water meadows along the River Avon produced early feed for sheep before the spring pastures were ready.*

plants — including white and purple violets, and lords and ladies — and a wealth of insects, including many butterflies and grasshoppers. Wiltshire snails are a famous local delicacy, served with garlic butter.

Rain soaking through the chalk emerges as springs and creates the pure chalk streams and rivers, famous in this area for trout. Swans and wagtails can also be seen.

Until recent times March and April were difficult months for shepherds to feed their sheep. Winter hay had run out and the spring pasture was not ready. The solution was to create water meadows. These can be found in many counties but Wiltshire has particularly fine examples.

A system of trenches and drains was dug, leading off, then back to, a main river. The meadows were irrigated by running water onto them.

◄*One of the most attractive parts of Urchfont is by the pond. The village is surrounded by water-meadows and woodlands. The garden warbler (inset) winters in Africa.*

A rural walk in a little-known valley

Even today, the Vale of Pewsey is a quiet, secret place. Rich and fertile, this valley is about 12 miles (19.2 km) long and lies between the Marlborough Downs to the north and Salisbury Plain to the south.

Small villages are tucked away, half-concealed among lush meadows and woods. One of the most enchanting of these is Urchfont Ⓐ where this walk begins. A fine 14th-century church overlooks a pond surrounded by groups of thatched, half-timbered cottages and elegant brick-built Georgian houses. The path leads beside a small stream through woods, in a Nature Reserve carpeted with wild flowers, then over the fields to return along a green way, past the manor house.

In and around Urchfont village are deep, sunken lanes, overhung with flowers and ferns in spring and early summer. The route leads past

FACT FILE

- Urchfont, about 5 miles (8 km) south of Devizes

- Pathfinder 1201 (SU 05/15), grid reference SU 040571

  miles 0 1 2 3 4 5 6 7 8 9 10 miles
  kms 0 1 2 3 4 5 6 7 8 9 10 11 12 13 14 15 kms

- 2 ½ hours. Extra time is needed to explore the village and Nature Reserve

- No climbs, but careful navigation needed as there are few footpath signs. The not-so-nimble may need help to cross some stiles. Walking boots or wellingtons are recommended as the ground can be boggy. Overgrown in summer, when not recommended for young children

- P Beside the pond in Urchfont village, close to the church

- The Nag's Head pub serves meals

thatched cottages, with their old-fashioned gardens reaching, and growing into, the hedges. The village church is mainly 14th-century, with a 15th-century tower and porch. It has some rare 14th-century stained glass, fine stone vaulting and a 13th-century font.

In the village there is a tree Ⓑ that

▼*Green paths and sunken lanes are a feature of the Vale of Pewsey. The rich soil encourages wild flowers and ferns.*

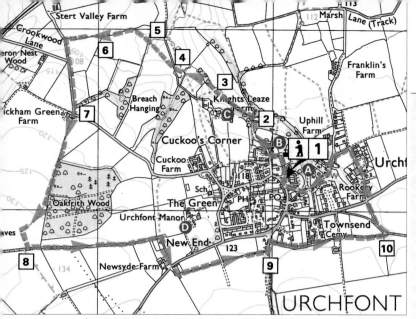

URCHFONT

The walk begins at the pond in Urchfont Village Ⓐ. From the B3098, drive through part of the village in the direction of the church. The pond is on your right.

1 With the pond on your right walk straight ahead in the direction of the church towards a large, brick house roofed with stone slabs. Walk down the lane that runs just to the right of the house — you will see the church beyond. Follow the narrow path straight ahead that runs to the left of the church tower. Turn left when you come to a lane and follow it to a crossing where you will see a footpath sign reading 'Stert Valley 1¼' pointing right. The tree Ⓑ, planted to commemorate King George V's silver jubilee, is on this corner. Turn right down the concreted sunken lane which leads down to a stream and iron gate.

2 Just before the stream, you will see a narrow path with a dense canopy of foliage leading through the woods — a National Nature Reserve Ⓒ on your left. Follow this with the stream on your right. Cross the stile and walk straight on, along a very overgrown path to a stile in a barbed-wire fence. Go past a wooden bridge on your right, to another stile that you will see on top of a rise to the right.

3 Cross the stile and walk over the field ahead, bearing left away from the stream towards a wooden stile in a dip next to a telegraph pole. Cross this, walk over a concrete bridge over the stile at the other side and walk up the field ahead to a wooden stile you will see on top of a rise. Cross this and walk straight over a farm track to cross the stile on the other side.

4 Turn right and walk round the edge of the field. There is no path here and when a crop is in the field it is planted up to the fence. Keep the fence on your right. Bear left (stream on right) to a wooden stile on your right. The right of way goes straight across this field, but it is much easier to walk round the edge when the field is sown.

5 Cross the stile and turn right to walk to the hedge. Now bear left along the edge of the field (hedge on your right). Again the right of way goes straight over the field, but the route indicates walking round it.

6 You come to a farm track with a barbed-wire fence breaking the line of the hedge. Turn right, then immediately left, with the hedge close on your left, through a field that often has cattle in it. At the end of the field, turn left through a gate which leads to a lane. Bear left along the lane keeping straight on when the lane becomes metalled. Passing the farm buildings on your left, you can see the white horse of Alton Barves across the Vale of Pewsey.

7 When the lane bends sharply left, look straight ahead and you will see the entrance to a farm. Just to the left of the farm entrance is a small white stile. Cross a ditch and another stile. When planted, the crop is up to the fence and walking can be difficult here. Keep straight on, past the house on your right, towards a wood — Oakfrith Wood.

Go through a gate and keep straight on with a wood and electric fencing on your left.

8 Climb the ladder, which is slippery and within dense undergrowth in summer, into a green lane. Turn left to follow this way. You will see Urchfont Manor Ⓓ over the fields. Follow the lane as it bends right (ignore the By-Way sign) to the B3098. Cross the road and follow the track ahead as it bears left to become a deep sunken path beside the fields. Keep straight on over the first crossing track.

9 At this crossing lane turn left for a short distance, then right to continue along the sunken path. Keep straight on over the next crossing track keeping the 'Private Land' sign on your right.

10 At the next junction, a track leads right into a field over a grassy bank where you will see the path continuing. Do not cross to it, but turn left and walk down the lane to the B3098. Cross the road and walk up Crooks Lane opposite. At a crossing lane, turn left, and then left again at the next crossing lane. Keep to the lane as it dips and climbs between high banks, often colourful with wild flowers, and past thatched cottages. Return to the pond in the centre of the village, and the start of the walk.

◄*Thatched cottages on Urchfont village green. Thatching is one of the oldest building crafts in Britain.*

commemorates the silver jubilee of King George V. It was planted in 1936 by a villager, Mary Alexander, who was born on 3rd January 1835, making her 101 years old on the day of the tree-planting ceremony.

Early in the year, the Nature Reserve Ⓒ is full of snowdrops with carpets of anemones. Celandines and bluebells bloom in May.

Urchfont Manor Ⓓ dates from the time of William and Mary. It was once owned by the statesman William Pitt the Elder (1708-1778).

UP WICK HILL

From an old-world village on a nature trail cupped in downland

Far from crowds, through leafy lanes, woods, meadows and downs, this walk takes in tranquil pastoral scenes that could have come straight from the pages of a Thomas Hardy novel. Bremhill **Ⓐ**, at the start of the route, is a village with an ancient church on a hill that overlooks an old market cross and a single street of honey-coloured stone cottages.

The walk climbs gently to follow the top of the downs giving marvellous views for over 1 mile (1.6 km).

This is a good area for wild flowers. In the spring the woods are full of bluebells and heavy with the scent of wild garlic. The lanes are embanked with cow parsley, ragged robin and wild arum. The hedgerows are alive with small birds — wrens, chaffinches, long-tailed tits — pheasants stalk the meadows and larks and hawks hover over the downs.

REVEREND RHYMES

Many of Bremhill's old stone cottages have thatched roofs. The 13th-century church has a porch with a fan-vaulted roof and a rare, ornately carved stone pulpit dating from the 14th century. If the church is locked,

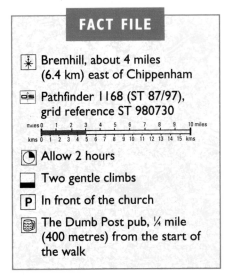

FACT FILE

- ✳ Bremhill, about 4 miles (6.4 km) east of Chippenham

- 🗺 Pathfinder 1168 (ST 87/97), grid reference ST 980730

  miles 0 1 2 3 4 5 6 7 8 9 10 miles
  kms 0 1 2 3 4 5 6 7 8 9 10 11 12 13 14 15 kms

- ◗ Allow 2 hours

- ▬ Two gentle climbs

- 🅿 In front of the church

- 🍺 The Dumb Post pub, ¼ mile (400 metres) from the start of the walk

the key can be obtained from the shop opposite. The Reverend William Lisle Bowles (1762-1850) was rector here from 1804 until his death. His poems were admired by the Romantic poets, S T Coleridge and William Wordsworth, who visited him at the Old Vicarage. One of his poems, dedicated to an old soldier, is carved on the wall of the church close to the south porch. Like Wordsworth, he wrote about country folk at a time when they were not considered worthy of notice. He had a habit of keeping sheep with their bells tuned in thirds and fifths. Their descendants still graze in the shadow of the church tower. Further

▲*Bremhill is a quiet village with literary associations. Cornflowers (inset) are seldom seen in corn fields due to modern farming methods.*

along the route there is a viewpoint **Ⓑ** from the crest of the down and the panorama can be appreciated all along the ridge. You can see over the north Wiltshire plain to the Cotswold hills and it is possible to see the curve of the horizon.

Along the ridge, the carved figure

THE WALK

BREMHILL

This circular walk begins near Bremhill's church, beside the minor road that runs through Bremhill village Ⓐ.

1 Walk past the market cross and down the village street (the church is behind you). Follow the country lane as it dips into a valley then climbs a little through rolling pastoral countryside. The lane then dips to meet another lane in front of a small thatched cottage.

2 Turn left here and follow the lane past the turning for Charlcutt in the direction of Tytherton.

3 When the lane bends sharply left round some stone farm buildings, leave the lane and keep straight on along a track and through a gate. This becomes a green field path with a fence on the right.

4 After the iron gate on the crest of the down there is a viewpoint Ⓑ ahead. Do not go through the gate, but turn left and walk along the crest of the down with a fence and a small wood on your right. Follow the ridge through a wooden gate and several iron gates, past Maud Heath's monument Ⓒ.

5 You will see a house on your left. Go through an iron gate, across the minor road to Bremhill

Wick, past the inscribed stone Ⓓ on your right and through the iron gate ahead. Follow the crest of the down again, through more iron gates, where there is a plantation on your right, until you see a little wood ahead. Bear left as you come to the wood to leave the field through an iron gate and meet the country lane at the top of Bencroft Hill. Turn left along the lane.

6 Pass Bencroft Farm on your left and a short distance further on look very carefully for a narrow earth path on your right, which can be slightly overgrown at the entrance. There is a metal gate directly opposite. Leave the lane and turn right down this narrow path, which

leads downhill through a small wood to bring you to a wooden gate.

7 From the gate walk down the field towards a wood ahead. Just before the gate into the wood, bear left along a faint path across the fields, which are quite wild and become overgrown in summer. Follow this, with two small woods on your right, through a wooden gate in a fence. The track leads to a gate that opens onto a country lane. Turn left and walk up the lane, passing the Dumb Post pub on your right.

8 There is another lane just past the Dumb Post. Turn right along it for a short distance and in front of the Dumb Post you will see, on the left-hand side of

the lane, a gravel track with a house close beside it on the right. The track looks private but is a public right-of-way. Walk past the garage on your right, squeeze through a small opening in the wooden fence beside a gate, and keep straight on along the top of the field (hedge on your left) through two metal gates. Follow the field path and cross a stile. Skirt the field to the right next to the fence by the tennis court. Ahead you will see the tower of Bremhill's church. Cross to the tower, go through a gate in the churchyard wall and look right to see the Old Vicarage. A path on your left will lead you round the church to the minor road where you turn right for the square.

◄ Maud Heath died a widow, leaving money to build a raised path from Wick Hill to Chippenham so that people could walk to market dry shod. The monument to her was erected in 1838.

of Maud Heath sits proudly on top of her monument Ⓒ, looking towards Chippenham on the plain below. In 1474 she left all her money to build a causeway from the hill, where she sits, to the town. The

causeway leads from Wick Hill and passes through Langley Burrell. A poem by William Lisle Bowles is inscribed on the column. Bowles' inscription reads:
'From this Wick Hill begins the Praise/Of Maud Heath's Gift to these Highways'.

There is another inscription commemorating Maud Heath's gift. This appears on the inscribed stone Ⓓ situated on the top of Wick Hill.

▲ *A chalk ridge overlooks farmland around Whiteparish where the chalk-loving pyramidal orchid (left) can be found. The pyramid-shaped flower cluster attracts butterflies and moths.*

A stroll along a ridge path with views of three counties

Panoramic views from a magnificent ridge path that the route follows for almost 3 miles (4.8 km) are the outstanding feature of this walk. The high chalk ridge runs east of the River Avon south of Salisbury, giving splendid views over the city and Salisbury Plain beyond. The route climbs from the small village of Whiteparish Ⓐ through gentle undulating countryside to the highest point on the ridge near Pepperbox Hill. The hill, crowned by its oddly shaped tower, is owned by the National Trust who preserve and maintain the natural chalk downland noted for its wild flowers, birds and butterflies.

Whiteparish is a pleasant village set in a shallow vale of undulating farmland and small copses north of the massed woods of the New Forest. The vale, with cultivated fields bordered by thick hedges, contrasts with the high ridge of chalk downland that forms its northern boundary.

From viewpoint Ⓑ on the ridge there are panoramic views over three counties — Wiltshire, Hampshire and Dorset. Across the Avon to the west is Odstock Down. The city of Salisbury lies almost at the foot of the ridge, distinguished by the soaring spire of its magnifi-

cent cathedral. Southampton and the Isle of Wight are to the south.

Grimstead Beeches Ⓒ is an old wood with a footpath through it which joins the ridge path. Opposite the wood is the grid point marking the highest point on the ridge, 515 feet (157 metres).

JACOBEAN FOLLY

The Pepperbox Ⓓ is a curious Jacobean tower, also known as Eyre's Folly. Built of brick in 1606, it is octagonal with a pyramid-shaped roof. It may have been built as an eye-catcher — according to legend, Gyles Eyre, a local landowner, was envious of the high towers of Longford Castle and built this tower on the hill so he could look down on his neighbours. Or it may have been designed to enable ladies to observe falconry and the hunt from the room in the upper storey.

The grassed slopes of Pepperbox Hill are mown by the National Trust to encourage bee and pyramidal orchids, harebells, vetches and other wild flowers. During the Iron Age the chalk down was cultivated, but today the Trust plants berried shrubs including junipers, encouraging birds and thus making it a good area for bird watching.

FACT FILE

- ✳ Whiteparish, about 8 miles (13 km) south-east of Salisbury

- 🗺 Pathfinder 1263 (SU 22/32), grid reference SU 246236

  miles 0 1 2 3 4 5 6 7 8 9 10 miles
  kms 0 1 2 3 4 5 6 7 8 9 10 11 12 13 14 15 kms

- 🕐 Allow 3 hours

- ▬ One long but gentle climb. Farmland around Whiteparish can be muddy in wet weather; strong shoes are recommended

- 🅿 Beside the church in Whiteparish

- Ⓣ Whiteparish is on the Salisbury—Romsey bus route

- 🏛 All facilities in Whiteparish, including a pub

THE WALK

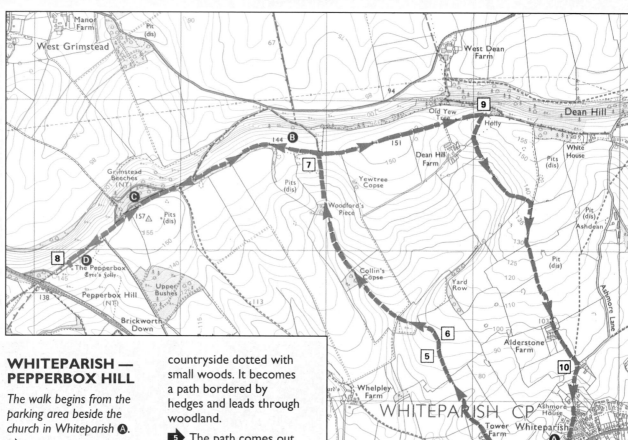

WHITEPARISH — PEPPERBOX HILL

The walk begins from the parking area beside the church in Whiteparish Ⓐ.

1 From the parking area turn left and walk down Redlynch Road for about 150 yards (135 metres) until you see two footpath signs on the right.

2 Do not follow the wider, more obvious track but turn right as indicated by the wooden fingerpost for Dean Hill. Between two houses there is a narrow path. Keep to this, cross the stile and continue with the hedge on your left until you reach a stile on your left and two footpath signs.

3 Cross the rickety stile and turn right to follow a narrow, overgrown path. This meets a track and continues to the main road, the A27.

4 Cross the road and follow the bridleway immediately ahead, which is a lane at this point. The lane climbs gently to give views of undulating

countryside dotted with small woods. It becomes a path bordered by hedges and leads through woodland.

5 The path comes out of the wood into open country through gateposts (gate missing). Navigate carefully here. Turn right and continue for about 100 yards (90 metres).

6 Turn left here. There is a small yellow arrow (footpath sign) on your right. Continue up the side of the field with the hedge on your right. The path climbs a little more steeply and curves — keep the hedge on your right.

7 Towards the top of the ridge the path is crossed by the ridge path. Turn left and follow this path to the viewpoint Ⓑ to enjoy the magnificent views. Continue past the old woods of Grimstead Beeches Ⓒ until you cross open chalk downland and see the curiously shaped tower called the Pepperbox Ⓓ just to the

left of the path.

8 After visiting the Pepperbox, retrace your steps along the ridge path. Alternatively, there are parallel paths through Grimstead Beeches. Stay on the path, past the previous joining point to meet a metalled lane. Bear left uphill away from Dean Hill Farm.

9 Continue along the metalled lane until you see a small wood on your right. Turn right down a track just before the wood and continue with the wood, and later a tall hedge, on your left. Walk on downhill, straight over a

crosstrack where there are views east towards the New Forest, with Southampton on the horizon. Walk straight over a farmyard and keep straight on.

10 The track meets a lane. (At this point you will see a bridleway sign for Dean Hill pointing back the way you have come.) Turn right and walk down the hill. When the road divides bear right into Whiteparish village. The church is on the opposite side of the A27. Cross the road to the church and the starting point of the walk.

WILTSHIRE

designated a conservation area.

Castle Combe's magnificent church of St Andrew dates back to the 12th century. Old stone cottages cluster round a 14th-century market cross and rows of weavers' cottages stand beside the By Brook which powered the fulling mills in medieval times. Today, the village contains more restaurants and inns than industry.

The nearby settlement of Long Dean ❸ is very small — a handful of

◀ *Castle Combe prospered from the cloth industry during medieval times. In Roman, Irish and many European mythologies, the houseleek (inset) protects houses from lightning.*

A walk centred on one of the most attractive villages in England

This walk starts from Castle Combe ❹, a picture-book village built of honey-coloured Cotswold stone framed by wooded hillsides. Many of the houses are hundreds of years old and all are listed as ancient monuments.

The walk follows the course of a stream along a terraced hillside and through two other attractive villages before returning by an alternative route, which gives lovely views of remote hidden valleys. The countryside here is so rich in wild flowers and birds that it has been

FACT FILE

⚹ Castle Combe, about 8 miles (12.8 km) north-west of Chippenham

🗺 Pathfinder 1168 (ST 87/97), grid reference ST 841769

miles 0 1 2 3 4 5 6 7 8 9 10 miles
kms 0 1 2 3 4 5 6 7 8 9 10 11 12 13 14 15 kms

◕ 2½ hours

▬ One very short climb. An ideal family walk

🅿 In Castle Combe village car park

🍴 Inns, restaurants and all facilities in Castle Combe village
♿

▲ *Long Dean Mill can be seen nestling in the verdant valley where the hamlet of Long Dean is situated.*

THE WALK

CASTLE COMBE – LONG DEAN

The walk begins in Castle Combe village Ⓐ *car park. Follow the signs to the village car park.*

1 From the car park, turn right down the road and right again at the junction. After the first houses, you will see a footpath sign on the right to Nettleton Shrub. Follow this past the school, turn left over a stile and continue until you come to some high stone walls. Follow the stepped lane under a small arch down into Castle Combe village under Archway Cottage. Bear right past the market cross and over the bridge. Continue down the road with the By Brook on your left. Ignore the first bridge on your left, but turn left over the second bridge, which is built of stone and known locally as 'The Roman Bridge'. Turn immediately right following the footpath sign for Long Dean. The wooded valley is now on your right. Cross a concrete step stile. The path gains a little height and is terraced along the hillside. Keep to the main path and cross a stone step stile. (The path occasionally alters course a little to avoid muddy patches). It then becomes a narrow lane leading past the mill into the hamlet of Long Dean Ⓑ.

2 Follow the main path as it bears right through the hamlet to cross a bridge over the By Brook.

The path continues uphill as a sunken track. Follow it through a gate and into a wood. Leave the wood (the path is rather faint) and keep straight on towards a minor road ahead.

3 About 100 yards (90 metres) before the minor road, look carefully for a path on the left. Follow this as it crosses the hillside diagonally towards the minor road. Cross the stile and turn left down the minor road towards Ford village.

4 When the road meets the A420, turn right along the footpath for a short distance. Just past the bus shelter turn right up a little track called Park Lane. Follow it to a stile.

5 Cross the stile into a field and turn immediately right along a narrow path, which soon becomes wider as it enters a wood.

6 Careful navigation is needed here. After about 75 yards (67 metres) bear right into the field at the side of the wood, keeping the wood on your left. (The field slopes down to the stream on your right.) Keep straight on (heading north) and look ahead to see a clear white path climbing the hillside. Reaching it requires careful navigation. As you reach a wooded area the path divides. Do not follow either of the obvious tracks but turn immediately right for a short distance to a stile on your left. Cross this, bear right over a plank bridge and climb uphill along the white path seen earlier.

7 The path leads through the wood, then bears to the left (away from the fence) to climb diagonally up the hillside to a tall waymarked post on the top of the hill. Continue along the top of the hill with the hedge on your right. There are good views from here of remote wooded valleys. To enter the wood, cross a stile, but just before this look across the valley to the top of Truckle Hill where a stone barn marks the site of a Roman villa Ⓒ. The path dips through the wood to meet a minor road. Turn left and follow it to a Y-junction.

8 Continue left along the road to North Wraxall. After about 50 yards (45 metres) ignore a stone stile on the right and continue for another 30 yards (27 metres) to a barbed wire gate (easy to open) on the right. Go through it and bear left along a little track which becomes a clearer path leading downhill through a wood to the minor road to Castle Combe. Turn left and walk past the bridge to the parking area.

cottages set in a remote valley. Virtually unspoilt, it looks as if it is straight from the pages of a Thomas Hardy novel. The houses are linked by an old stony track, overgrown with grass, and their flower-filled gardens contrast with the dark wooded hillsides.

Further on the walk it is possible to see the site of the Roman Villa Ⓒ on Truckle Hill. It is off the route, but to visit it, follow the track that leads off the North Wraxall road. Just over 1 mile (1.6 km) west of Truckle Hill runs the Fosse Way, the great Roman Road that crosses the Cotswolds and connects Lincoln with Bath.

Through the Vale of Pewsey to hills and ancient earthworks

The fertile Vale of Pewsey lies between the Marlborough Downs and Salisbury Plain. Even today it is quiet and remote. Its attractive villages are tucked away among narrow, twisting lanes, undisturbed by 20th-century bustle. The whole area is marked by signs of Bronze and Iron Age settlements.

Rich farmland, canal banks and open downs provide a wide variety of bird and plant life. Kestrels hover over the downs, and the banks of the canal are particularly rich in flowers such as flag irises.

All Cannings **A**, mentioned in the *Domesday Book* as 'Caninge', is one of the prettiest villages of the Pewsey Vale. Attractive cottages of all dates — many half-timbered and thatched — are set behind grassy banks and around greens, and are often half-hidden by their overflowing gardens. All Cannings won 'best kept village' awards in 1985 and

1988. The church of All Saints dates back to Norman times and has a fascinating little wooden door halfway up the wall of the north transept. It originally led to the rood screen. The Rev T A Methuen was rector here for 60 years, and built the village school beside the church in 1833.

S T Coleridge, poet and essayist, visited Methuen at the rectory **B** in 1817. This was the year in which the poet published his autobiography, entitled *Biographia Literaria*. With his appreciation of nature, he must have delighted in the beauty of the Vale.

RESTORED CANAL

The recently restored Kennet and Avon Canal **C** is a modern success story. Left to decay after the last working boat passed through it in 1951, teams of volunteers have now restored its pumping stations, locks and aqueducts.

Great sheep fairs, to which shepherds brought their flocks from the surrounding area, were once held on Tan Hill **D**. The view is marvellous, particularly over the Vale of Pewsey, which is dotted with hamlets.

The Wansdyke **E** is a splendid

▲*The view from Wansdyke takes in a sweep of farmland, tumuli and other earthworks on the surrounding downs. The brown argus butterfly (inset) may be seen here between April and August.*

FACT FILE

All Cannings in the Vale of Pewsey, 5 miles (8km) east of Devizes

Pathfinder 1185 (SU 06/16), grid reference SU 069616

miles 0 1 2 3 4 5 6 7 8 9 10 miles
kms 0 1 2 3 4 5 6 7 8 9 10 11 12 13 14 15 kms

Allow 2½ hours

One steady climb of about 1 mile (1.6km). Walking shoes with a strong grip are recommended, as chalk can be slippery when wet

Beside the church in All Cannings or in a parking area beside the green

The King's Arms pub

Shop and tea rooms in All Cannings (cream teas)

THE WALK

ALL CANNINGS – WANSDYKE

The walk begins by the church in All Cannings Ⓐ.

1 Opposite the entrance to the church you will see a footpath sign. Follow this between the pink-washed rectory Ⓑ and some thatched cottages. Follow the path down a slight slope and over a stream to a field. Turn right along the field edge, keeping fences and hedges on your right.

2 After the path bears left, look carefully for a small path leading through the hedge on the right. Take this to cross the canal Ⓒ by an iron swing-bridge. Keep straight on, to a tarmacked lane into Allington village.

3 Follow the lane straight over the crossroads for about 200 yards (180m) and turn right down a grassy path, which leads to a minor road. Turn left for about 50 yards (45m), then right following the 'Bridleway only' sign on the gate. Climb up the downs, over cattle grids, to the top of the hill. The plateau to the east was the site of the Tan Hill Ⓓ sheep fair. The path dips down to cross the Wansdyke ditch. Turn right and walk beside the Wansdyke for about 100 yards (90m). Turn right to cross over the Wansdyke Ⓔ, go over a stile and keep straight on over the top of the down with a fence on your right.

4 Ahead of you at the next stile you can see Rybury Camp Ⓕ. Cross the stile and, leaving the fence, bear a little left to follow a terraced path leading down to the foot of Rybury Hill, crossing another stile.

5 When you come to a gate leading to cultivated land, the right-of-way is across the field. If there is no obvious path, take the path to the left around the field, keeping a hedge on your right. The path bears round to the right. After about 50 yards (45m) the hedge becomes a double row of hawthorn bushes and you will see a stile on your right. Cross this and turn left to follow the path between bushes. Go through a gate and follow the wide, grassy lane ahead to a minor road.

6 The right-of-way is immediately over the road, past some farm buildings. Turn right in front of the farmhouse, through a gate. Bear a little right and walk diagonally across the field ahead to a stile in the right-hand corner. Turn left over the stile and keep on with the hedge on your right. At the point where some cables cross the path, just past a supporting post, turn right and walk along the edge of the field (hedge on right). When the path meets a wide bridleway, turn left and follow this to cross Woodway Bridge, over the canal. Go straight ahead, through a gate and over a field, towards All Cannings. Bear left, then right, to walk through the village to the start.

bank and ditch, stretching 50 miles (80km) from Savernake Forest to Dundry Hill, south of Bristol. It possibly dates from Celtic times and marked the territorial boundary of a regional tribe or chieftain. Country people later could only attribute the making of such long and useless ditches to the Devil, so they called it 'Woden's Dyke' (the Anglo-Saxon war god Woden was identified with the Devil); in time this became abbreviated to 'Wansdyke'.

Rybury Camp Ⓕ is a well-preserved, Iron Age hill-fort. It stands out from the line of the Downs and must have been a fine vantage point, dominating the Vale of Pewsey.

◀ *The Norman church and some half-timbered cottages in All Cannings are recorded in the* **Domesday Book.**

AVON HAVEN

WILTSHIRE

A beautiful canal and riverside walk in the heart of the Avon Valley

Bradford-on-Avon **Ⓐ**, where the walk begins, is an enchanting riverside town, whose streets are packed with elegant, sandy-coloured, stone-built Georgian houses. There are also medieval cottages, a 14th-century bridge with a domed chapel and perhaps the finest Saxon church in the country.

SAXON CHURCH

There have been settlements here since the Iron Age, and there are Roman roads and villas in these parts too, but it was the Saxons who gave Bradford its greatest treasure. St Laurence's Church was founded in the 7th century by St Aldhelm, first Abbot of Malmesbury, when he established a monastery here. The

▲ Rediscovered in 1856, St Laurence's Church had been hidden by buildings and used as a school and a home. Flowers of wet meadows (left) can be found growing at Barton Farm.

FACT FILE

✴ Bradford-on-Avon, 2½ miles (4km) north-west of Trowbridge

▭ Pathfinders 1184 (ST 86/96) and 1200 (ST 85/95), grid reference ST 824607

miles 0 1 2 3 4 5 6 7 8 9 10 miles
kms 0 1 2 3 4 5 6 7 8 9 10 11 12 13 14 15 kms

◕ Allow 3 hours to a full day

▭ Along a towpath, country lanes and field tracks

P At start of walk

T BR from London, Bath and Bristol. Well served by bus and coach

🍺 Pubs in Bradford-on-Avon and
🍽 Avoncliff. Teas at Barton Farm and Westwood

WC By car park and at Barton Farm Country Park

⌂ Barton Farm buildings are open every day in summer; Westwood Manor on Sunday, Tuesday and Wednesday afternoons in summer

---

church is almost completely Saxon, and has a very high and narrow chancel arch, as well as rounded windows and arcading.

In medieval times, Bradford was a centre of the cloth trade, and the rows of weavers' and spinners' cottages date from that period. Church

House and the Old Priory date from the 15th century, while the Chantry, with its fine Classical facade, was built a century later. Another building of note to be found here is The Hall, built in 1610 by clothier John Hall, which has mullioned windows and an attractive porch.

The town prospered in the 17th and 18th centuries, as the cloth it produced became famous, and a

THE WALK

BRADFORD-ON-AVON – WESTWOOD

The walk starts from the car park just north of the station in Bradford-on-Avon **Ⓐ**.

1 Walk away from the A363 and up the steps signposted 'To the Swimming Pool' at the far end of the car park. Continue left past the swimming pool to the river bank and bear left along it. Keep straight on under a railway bridge and through a grassy picnic area, with Barton Farm **Ⓑ** and its tithe barn on your left.

weir **Ⓓ** and an aqueduct.

3 Immediately before the aqueduct, turn right following the sign 'Towpath to Limpley Stoke'. After a few paces, turn left in front of the Cross Guns pub, following the towpath sign. After passing under the aqueduct, turn immediately left up some steps to a lane. Follow it uphill for about 100 yards (90m).

4 Where the lane bends sharp left, with a private road off to your right, go through a wooden gate straight ahead. Follow the woodland path uphill, going

this meets a road, keep straight on. The road turns right, but again keep straight on towards a row of garages. Take the path ahead, to the left of the garages, and past a barrier, to reach a minor road.

6 Turn left along the footpath beside the road. After 50 yards (45m), climb some steps to the right of the road, squeeze through the stile and follow a field

crossing a stile, and along the field path ahead. Cross another stile and keep straight on to a third stile.

9 Cross this stile and turn left along a faint, crossing path, keeping a hedge on your left. The path bears right, away from the hedge, towards a stile by a footpath sign. Cross it onto the road.

10 Cross the road and follow a 'Barton Farm' footpath sign through a gate to your right. Follow the path straight on over a stile, downhill, then over a waymarked stile and continue, keeping a hedge on your left.

11 When you come to a wire fence, turn right and walk downhill for about a 100 paces until you see a stile with a yellow waymark arrow on your left. Cross the stile and bear left round the top of the field to an iron stile.

12 Do not cross the stile but turn right and walk diagonally down the field towards the canal. Cross a stile and, after another stile and a wooden footbridge, you come to the footpath along the canal bank. Follow it until you reach the swingbridge.

13 Turn left over the swingbridge, cross the canal towpath you followed earlier and take the path ahead, which leads down to the river. Bear right along the riverside path, which brings you back to the car park. To visit the Saxon church, turn left out of the car park entrance and cross another car park to the river. Cross the footbridge and go past the large church. As you walk uphill, the Saxon church is on your right.

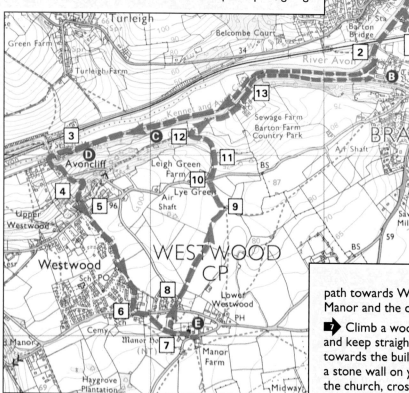

2 Leave the riverside and cross the grass towards the barn. Go up some steps to its right, marked by a yellow arrow, then turn right to follow the towpath of the Kennet and Avon Canal **Ⓒ**. Keep to the path, continuing past a swingbridge, until you reach some old mills by a

straight on at an intersection, past a stile to a lane. Go straight on until you reach a minor road.

5 Cross over and turn left, following the sign immediately to the right for Bobbin Park. When the broad path bears right, keep straight on along the narrow path ahead. When

path towards Westwood Manor and the church.

7 Climb a wooden stile and keep straight on towards the buildings, with a stone wall on your left. At the church, cross the churchyard and go through the gate. Westwood Manor **Ⓔ** is on your left. From the manor, retrace your steps to the wooden stile. Do not cross it, but turn right, alongside a stone wall. Go through a gate and cross over the Lower Westwood road, along the lane ahead.

8 When the lane turns left keep straight on,

Avon at Bristol. The canal was completed in 1810 and was soon packed with traffic carrying local coal, iron, stone and agricultural products east to London.

NEW LEASE OF LIFE

When a new railway line opened between London and Bristol in 1841, the canal fell into disrepair. In 1962, the Kennet and Avon Canal Trust was set up to organize the largest civil engineering project ever

◀*The 14th-century bridge over the Avon, with a domed chapel for pilgrims; in the 17th century this became a lock-up. The Kennet and Avon Canal (below) is now a navigable waterway once more.*

wealth of fine Georgian buildings sprang up. The mills built in the 18th century have recently been restored by the company whose premises they now are.

MONASTERY FARM

Initially, the walk leads south out of the town and along the river to Barton Farm Country Park ❸. For 500 years, the buildings here formed part of a huge farm belonging to and supplying the nearby monastery. The farmhouse, granary and byres

have been restored and now form a complex of galleries and craft shops. There is also a magnificent 14th-century tithe barn.

From here you head westwards along the towpath of the Kennet and Avon Canal ❸. This beautifully restored waterway stretches a full 87 miles (139km) from the River Thames at Reading to the River

▼*The tithe barn, built by the Abbess of Shrewsbury, shows signs of ecclesiastical architecture in its design.*

undertaken by volunteers. Their work included the restoration of 86 derelict locks and 344 rotting lock gates, curing the leaks in the canal bed and rebuilding two crumbling aqueducts, pumping stations, wharves, bridges and other buildings. They also gave a new lease of life to the flight of 29 locks at Devizes, the longest series of locks in England. Today, the canal is once again a working waterway.

There is a rich variety of wildlife in and near the canal, including

chimney, suggesting that water power gave way to coal once the canal had been built.

The aqueduct, which carries the canal over the river, was built by John Rennie between 1796 and 1798. Now restored, it retains its elegant Georgian balustrades.

Heading south again, you come to Westwood Manor **E**, a small, stone-built 15th-century house with a friendly, homely atmosphere. It is now the property of the National Trust. Inside there are beautiful Jacobean plaster ceilings; outside, the fine gardens have some excellent topiary. The church at Westwood dates from the same period and has an impressive tower.

otters, mink, water voles and badgers. There are also many beautiful and unusual plants to be discovered growing along the banks and in the surrounding woods.

As you approach the hamlet of Avoncliff, the air is filled with the roar of water as it gushes over a great weir **D** that powered two mills. The one on the north bank, which still retains its breast-shot wheel, was once used for fulling (scouring) woven cloth. In the 19th century it became a flock mill, recycling old woollen materials. The other mill has a brick and stone

▲The River Avon flows through a shallow valley between woods and farmland to Avoncliff (above). An old fulling mill can be seen here by the weir. The 15th-century Westwood Manor (right) is noted for the neatly shaped topiary in its gardens.

The Development of Barns

The first written record of a barn dates from just after the Norman Conquest, though it is thought that the word has Saxon origins and described a place to store barley, which was the most popular grain.

Before steam-powered threshing machines made it possible to thresh in the fields, threshing was carried out inside massive barns. The sheaves that had been dried in the sun were heaped on the floor and beaten with flails. The draught through the huge doors at either side of the barn helped separate the wheat from the chaff. The spent straw was stored at one side of the barn for the cattle, and the grain was taken to the

Over 167 feet (50m) long and 30 feet (9m) wide, Barton Farm's tithe barn has massive walls and roof timbers and a stone-tiled roof.

granary. Barns were also used as sheep shearing sheds.

A tithe (or tenth) was a levy, comprising of a tenth of all produce, that had to be paid to the church. Tithe barns, which were often impressive buildings, were built to store these levies.

The barn at Bradford-on-Avon, one of the largest in England, was fashioned out of beautifully finished stone. The roof has fine oak timbers, with upper and lower collar beams on massive curved supports that are let into the wall. The huge doors of feathered oak planks are held by long iron hinges fixed by nails with huge heads. Light filters in through narrow slits like those of a medieval castle — indeed this impressive barn was once used as the set for Nottingham Castle in a film about Robin Hood.

Beyond this, the route turns south-west along the top of the downs. It runs above a large dry valley, a typical feature of the chalk downland, that was formed in the Ice Ages. Though the ice sheets did not quite reach this far south, the ground was frozen solid for much of the year. Rainwater ran off the frozen soil, carving out valleys. When the climate warmed again, the

◄*On the return route, a track descends from White Sheet Hill to the farmland in Wylye Valley. The chalkhill blue (inset) is a declining downland species that flies in July and August.*

FACT FILE

Kingston Deverill, 5 miles (8km) south of Warminster

Pathfinder 1240 (ST 83/93), grid reference ST 846370

miles 0 1 2 3 4 5 6 7 8 9 10 miles
kms 0 1 2 3 4 5 6 7 8 9 10 11 12 13 14 15 kms

4 hours

Clear paths on the chalk. Gentle climb at start, some steeper descents. Paths in the valley can be very muddy. Good footwear essential

P In the road near Kingston Deverill's church

None on route; several pubs in Mere, 3½ miles (5.6km) south-west of the start

A walk over the downs to an ancient trackway and a hilltop fort

This walk begins in the delightful village of Kingston Deverill, on the River Wylye, in a fold of the Wiltshire Downs. The Church of St Mary the Virgin ❹ was largely rebuilt in 1847 by Harriet, Marchioness of Bath, though the tower still contains some 14th-century work and a peal of six bells installed in 1731. Inside, there is an interesting pulpit, probably Flemish in origin, and a 14th-century wood carving of the Madonna and Child.

The route climbs uphill through the fields to Court Hill Plantation, one of several small patches of mixed woodland on the downs that have been planted as shelter for pheasants. The largest of these, Truncombe Wood ❸, is on the lower slopes below the path along the top of the escarpment.

▶*Behind Kingston Deverill's church is Kingston House, an interesting building with its own tower and a small spire.*

THE WALK

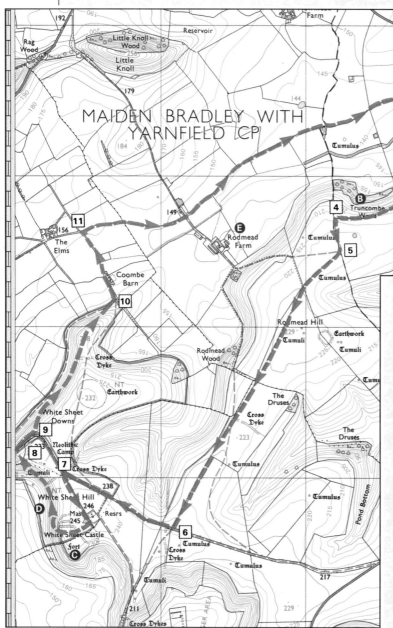

KINGSTON DEVERILL – WHITE SHEET HILL

The walk starts outside the church Ⓐ at Kingston Deverill, on the B3095.

1 Set off from beneath the yew tree that overhangs the churchyard wall. Walk away from the main road, with the main part of the village on your right. Where the road bears right, go straight ahead into a cul-de-sac.

2 Turn left along a concrete track and, at a barn, turn right to follow the track uphill.

3 At a small covered reservoir go right alongside Court Hill Plantation. At the end of the trees, turn left on a bridlepath along the top of the scarp slope. Pass the small wood of Peter's Penning then follow the fence on your left.

4 At the end of the field, above Truncombe Wood Ⓑ, turn left through a small gate and walk alongside the fence on your right.

5 At the top of a slight ascent, turn half right through a gap in the fence and walk straight across the field, making for a gate on the far side. Go through this and continue straight ahead across the top of the down, through several gates, until you reach Long Lane, a major cross-track

water sank through the porous chalk and the river disappeared.

The route then follows Long Lane, part of the ancient long-distance track known as Harrow Way, to reach White Sheet Hill. This gets its name from the colour of the chalk and from 'sceot', an old English word for a steep slope. This is part of the Stourhead Estate, which was given to the National Trust in 1946. The hill offers excellent views of

◀ *The view westwards along the scarp, looking over Truncombe Wood to Little Knoll, which lies north of the route.*

on White Sheet Hill.

6 Turn right along this ancient routeway, past the head of a large dry valley on your right. The track bears right round a dog-leg bend, passes over Cross Dyke, an ancient earthwork, and comes to a stile on the left.

7 Go over the stile onto the National Trust land and turn sharp left to follow the line of the fence. You cross the Dyke again then go on to the trig point in the Iron Age hill fort **C**. Turn right to walk across the fort then, at the top of the steep descent, turn to the right again to walk along the edge of the slope. There are a number of small terraces **D** below you on the left. Pass to the left of an old burial mound and make for another burial mound, where a stile is to be found.

8 Cross this stile and take a path steeply downhill until you reach another stile and a small, stony, National Trust car park. Turn right onto the road and right again to walk uphill along a stony track; this is Long Lane again. Shortly after you pass a milestone dated 1750, the Lane bends to the

right and there is a stile on the left.

9 Go over the stile and follow the level route along a trench. When the trench ends keep straight on over a faint path across the grass, and head towards the end of the hill. As you approach it, descend into the far corner of the field.

10 Go through the gate and turn left on the track which leads past Coombe Barn. Keep straight ahead until the track bends sharp left.

11 Turn right through a gate and into a field. The path leads straight ahead through two fields, crosses a track leading to Rodmead Farm **E**, and carries on through four more fields to a small wood. Keep straight on following field edges, crossing the track to Dairy Farm, until you come to a road.

12 Turn right and follow this road to Kingston Deverill **F**, taking the first right turn down into the village. Cross over the stream and turn left along its bank, passing Kingston House on your right. Turn right at the junction and right again to return to your starting point outside the church.

▲ *White Sheet Hill bears the marks of human occupation from many periods over the past 5,000 years. The banks and ditches of White Sheet Castle are about 2,500 years old. The tumulus (below), to the north of the castle, is around 4,000 years old.*

Stourhead and King Alfred's Tower over to the west.

The most dominant feature here now is a modern one, a radio mast, but there is plenty of evidence that this windswept hill was occupied in ancient times. White Sheet Castle **C**, a roughly triangular Iron Age hill fort, dating from around 500BC, looks out over the steep slopes to the south and west. There is just a single bank and ditch above the slopes, but three of them on the more vulnerable sides facing the level ground of the hilltop.

BEACON HILL

In the middle of the fort is a small circular mound. This may be the remains of an 18th-century animal shelter or the site of a beacon; this site is referred to as Beacon Hill on Saxton's 16th-century map of England and Wales.

Just below the fort, and probably dating from the same period, is the Cross Dyke, an embankment that may have been used to control stock or as a defensive barrier. Other signs of prehistoric farming can be seen on the western slopes in the form of terraces or strip lynchets **D**, which

▲This arched stone bridge crosses the River Wylye in Kingston Deverill.

were once narrow crop fields.

At the end of the walk along the hilltop are the remains of a Neolithic camp that originally had a causeway. This camp, approximately 5,000 years old, has almost disappeared, and the best view of its banks is from the large round barrow on its southern boundary. The barrow and the smaller burial mounds close by date from the Bronze Age, around 2,000BC.

GRAZING LAND

A small part of the hill is leased by the Wiltshire Trust for Nature Conservation and is protected as a Site of Special Scientific Interest. The Trust arranges for sheep to graze the area in winter to preserve the grassland and prevent it from being invaded by scrub. Rabbits also graze the sward and help keep the scrub at bay. A few blackthorn and hawthorn bushes provide song posts for birds

▼The site of an old quarry on White Sheet Hill is now managed as a nature reserve for downland species.

such as yellowhammers, which are particularly in evidence here.

Taller grasses grow in the summer, encouraging butterflies, including the rare chalkhill blue, as well as voles and other wildlife. Among the wild flowers are cowslips, bellflowers and horseshoe vetch — the main food plant of the chalkhill blue's caterpillar.

DOWNLAND FARM

The first part of the return walk crosses the lush farmland of the Wylye Valley. The site of Rodmead Farm ❺, at the foot of the steep slope, is a typical example of a downland farmhouse. Here there is a good water supply, shelter from the worst of the weather and easy access to the arable and dairy fields in the valley bottom and to the sheep pastures on the hillsides.

The final stretch of the walk is along the minor road from Maiden Bradley. It ends with a brief tour of Kingston Deverill ❻, which has two stone bridges over the Wylye and a small pond where the river has been widened. There are many lovely stone cottages, including two thatched ones, but the finest building is undoubtedly Kingston House, just behind the church.

Harrow Way

The Romans built the first hard-surfaced roads in Britain, but there is a network of even older routes criss-crossing the landscape. Part of this walk follows one of these ancient tracks, Harrow Way, which predates the Roman invasion by at least 500 years.

The route extended from Marazion, in Cornwall, to Kent. It was used primarily for the transport of Cornish tin. Alloyed with copper to make bronze, this was used for domestic implements and weapons, as well as jewellery. Like many of these old trade routes, Harrow Way tends to follow the high ground. The going was less muddy, and streams were easier to ford or bridge in their upper reaches than in the forested valley bottoms.

Harrow Way, also known as Hard Way, was used as a trade route by the Saxons, and sections of

Long Lane, a part of an ancient trade route and cattle drove, runs across the downs.

it were taken over as coaching roads in the 18th century. Tolls were charged for the upkeep of the road, and milestones, such as the one seen on the walk, were erected for the benefit of travellers using the coaches that linked Axmouth in Devon with Salisbury and the Thames Valley. Long Lane, the section of Harrow Way over White Sheet Hill, remained the main east-west road in the area until a new route, now the A303, was constructed at the foot of the hills.

Long Lane was then largely ignored by vehicle traffic, but was used as a drove road throughout the 19th century. Large flocks of sheep and cattle were driven along it to markets and fairs, notably at Yarnbury Castle, east of Wylye.

NELSON'S REWARD

◄*In the 18th century, Downton's medieval Moot was landscaped to include an amphitheatre and a pond, over which common blue damselflies (inset) can often be seen hovering.*

outside The White Horse pub, decorated with the heads of King John and Queen Isabella carved in wood.

The village unites each spring for the ancient Cuckoo Fair, said to mark the 'opening of the valley gates to let the cuckoo through'. The footpath entrance to the valley is by the 'iron bridge' **B** of 1820, so called because of its railings. The riverside path, which has a fine view of the church across the water, gives access to the 'floating meadows' **C**, which are popular with wildfowl.

FLOATING MEADOWS

The floating watermeadow system was an intricate form of irrigation that controlled river flooding by turning it to man's advantage. The scheme was devised in the early 17th century, and maintained until the beginning of this century. It is thought that Dutch prisoners held in Salisbury Cathedral's cloisters at the time of the Civil War may have provided the know-how.

The hamlet of Charlton **D**, on the edge of the floodplain, has sometimes been underwater, and today the eastern end of the churchyard is considered too damp for burials. The 1851, brick-built Church of All Saints is set to be converted inside to include a village hall. The Old Vicarage is the work of the Victorian ecclesiastical architect, William

▼*The floating watermeadow, a 17th-century irrigation system, was in common use until early this century.*

Meadows and a country house by an Avon Valley village

Downton is a village straggling the channels of the River Avon. In 1814, a nearby country house was given to Admiral Nelson's family as a reward for his services to the nation. This walk explores both.

Near the start is The Moot **A**, an earthwork dating from at least the time when King Stephen's brother, the Bishop of Winchester, built a castle there in the 12th century. The site was landscaped in the 1720s to include an amphitheatre, an attractive lily pond and a viewpoint.

DOUBLE MILL

The chemists at the centre of the village has an Egyptian-style doorway dating from 1826. A mill-stream runs by a working tannery and under a double mill; one for grist and the other for paper.

West of the Avon's main channel,

the village is known as The Borough. This is a 'new town', founded about 1205, with a wide street lined with small houses, including thatched cottages. The Borough's focal point is the cross

---

FACT FILE

⚹ Downton, 6 miles (9.6km) south of Salisbury

▭ Pathfinder 1262 (SU 02/12), grid reference SU 182215

| miles 0 | 1 | 2 | 3 | 4 | 5 | 6 | 7 | 8 | 9 | 10 miles |
| kms 0 | 1 2 3 4 5 6 7 8 9 10 11 12 13 14 15 kms |

◔ 2½ hours

▭ Riverside paths, a woodland track and field paths. Two short ascents

P In The Borough, in front of White Horse pub and Co-op

T Bus service from Bournemouth and Salisbury

🍺 Pubs and a fish and chip shop in 🍴 Downton

THE WALK

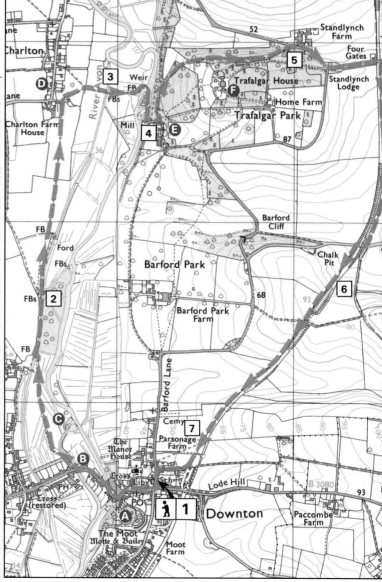

DOWNTON – CHARLTON

The walk begins at the library in Broad Lane, just off Downton's main street, on the eastern side of the village.

1 Turn right into the main street, passing The Moot **A** on your left. Follow the road to a bridge **B**. The riverside footpath is marked 'Charlton All Saints'. The path bears left and right before running over a water meadow **C**. Where the path bends left to a farm, keep ahead over grass to go left across a hidden footbridge by a pond. Turn right onto a concrete road.

2 On approaching a farmyard, leave the road to go over a stile on the right by a gate. Keep ahead over three fields linked by stiles. On the edge of Charlton **D** cross two stiles. A sign is marked 'Standlynch'. In the field, bear round to the right and go through a gap a few paces left of the fieldgate ahead. The path runs ahead on a raised grass causeway.

3 Cross the small footbridge and the main bridge. Keep forward by a ditch, but, after a few paces, switch banks by crossing a bridge before continuing in the same direction. Beyond a gate marked '1981', the path runs over three small footbridges and across the main Avon weir. Keep ahead on the narrow path to cross two small weirs and reach a mill. Turn left over the mill stream and up a sloping concrete path.

4 A slight detour following the path round to the right reveals a former chapel **E**. As the concrete path ends, turn sharp left up a hidden, short steep slope. A narrow path runs through the wood above the river, before bearing round to the right. Go over a stile at a gate to cross a sloping field with a view of Trafalgar House **F**. Beyond a gate, you head through woods. On meeting the mansion's driveway, go half left downhill to a road at Standlynch Farm.

5 Turn right. At Standlynch Lodge, turn left to Four Gates farmhouse. Cross the bridge ahead, and go immediately right along the side of two large fields. At a road, turn right through a tunnel then left to follow the other side of the railway.

6 The ground rises. Where the old line disappears into a tunnel, keep ahead over the brow of the hill, with a row of telegraph poles over to your right. Beyond a firm crosspath, look for a faint, narrow path running downhill towards the overgrown railway below. On meeting another path at a bend, keep ahead to climb up onto the bank. A narrow path runs along the track-bed. On approaching the village, turn sharp right to a stile. Turn left along the side of the railway and cross a stile by a cattle creep.

7 At a road bend, go straight ahead to turn right down an enclosed path, which soon has a fine view of the church tower. At the end, go left to return to the starting point.

Butterfield, and features his distinctive decorative brickwork.

From Charlton you cross the river channels to a mill. The boarded-up chapel **E** above the mill dates from 1677, when the estate here was known as Standlynch. In 1814, its name was changed to Trafalgar Park and the estate presented to Admiral Nelson's family, who continued to

▶ *This boarded-up chapel stands on the estate owned and occupied by Admiral Lord Nelson's family from 1814 to 1948.*

live here until 1948. The 18th-century mansion **F**, now owned by a hotel group, includes a Ganges Room with panelling from the ship and one of Nelson's telescopes.

INSPIRED RETURN

The final section of the walk follows the disused Salisbury to Wimborne railway line, which closed in 1965. As you return to Downton, which had a station for exactly a century, there are fine views, including one of Salisbury Cathedral's spire, 5 miles (8km) away.

◄*The grey-wether known as the Devil's Chair does not worry Avebury's sheep, which keep the surrounding grass short. Hoary plantain (inset) grows on grasslands that are less well grazed.*

FACT FILE

- ✳ Avebury, 6 miles (9.6km) west of Marlborough, just off the A4

- ▣ Pathfinders 1185 (SU 06/16) and 1169 (SU 07/17), grid reference SU 099699

  miles 0 1 2 3 4 5 6 7 8 9 10 miles
  kms 0 1 2 3 4 5 6 7 8 9 10 11 12 13 14 15 kms

- ◕ 4 hours

- ▭ Generally easy walking on level ground; some long, gentle slopes. Some sections on high, exposed pathways can be cold and muddy in winter

- P Car park on the A4361 just south-west of the village; small area beside the English Heritage shop

- T Buses from Swindon, Marlborough and Devizes, Tel. (01672) 513989

- ⛺ The Red Lion in Avebury serves food; restaurant by the Great Barn, Avebury

- ⛫ For details of the Alexander Keiller Museum, the Wiltshire Rural Life Museum and all other tourist information, Tel. (01672) 513989

Explore Britain's finest collection of prehistoric monuments

The largest henge and stone circle in the British Isles are set within a tranquil Wiltshire vale. A settlement sprang up within the standing stones and grew to become the village of Avebury.

In 1649, Avebury was 'discovered' by the diarist and author John Aubrey, who wrote, 'it does as much exceed in greatness the so renowned Stonehenge as a cathedral doth a parish church'. He had no idea who had constructed it, nor could he foresee its near destruction within the next century.

Fortunately, William Stukeley, an antiquarian, was equally captivated by the place, and spent seven years making meticulous notes and drawings of what he called 'that stupendous temple...the most august work at this day upon the globe of the earth'. He witnessed the toppling and smashing of many great stones by builders extending the village. His work provides an invaluable insight into what has been lost, and inspired a partial restoration of the site in the 20th century. It helped archaeologists to prove that the Avebury complex was a national monument when it was laid out 4,500 years ago.

Today, Avebury is listed by the United Nations as an International Heritage Site. Unlike Stonehenge, one can still roam freely here, touch the surviving stones and clamber up and down the banks. Walking around Avebury is an unforgettable experience. The surrounding downland is both beautiful and unspoilt, and the impact of the site increases as you leave cars and crowds behind and look back over the complex from the surrounding hills.

THE DEVIL'S WORK?

Medieval Christians saw Avebury as the work of the devil. Stukeley's drawings show that stones were arranged in the form of a serpent passing through the main circle. At Avebury's church, where the walk

▶ *The ditch around Avebury's henge was 60 feet (18m) deep when dug. Since then, it has filled in to half that depth.*

THE WALK

AVEBURY – EAST KENNET – OVERTON DOWN

The starting point of the walk is by Avebury's church.

1 Go along the lane to the henge and stone circle **A**. Turn right and go anti-clockwise round the circle. Just before it is crossed by the B4003, turn right along the Stone Avenue **B**. Return to the henge, and complete the circle. Turn right along the lane you followed from the church, then immediately left along an unmarked lane which takes you to a car park.

2 At the A4361, follow signs to Silbury Hill and West Kennet Long Barrow. Continue along the banks of the Kennet, past Silbury Hill **C**. Cross the A4 and continue ahead to West Kennet Long Barrow **D**. Retrace your steps, downhill to the stile below an oak tree at the bottom of the slope. Here turn right and follow the field boundary.

3 Cross a stile and follow a short track. Cross a metalled road, go over the stile and follow the cattle track to the far fence. Take the left-hand stile of two and cross the field to a jump replacing a stile. Continue, over another stile, to a lane. Turn left to reach a road.

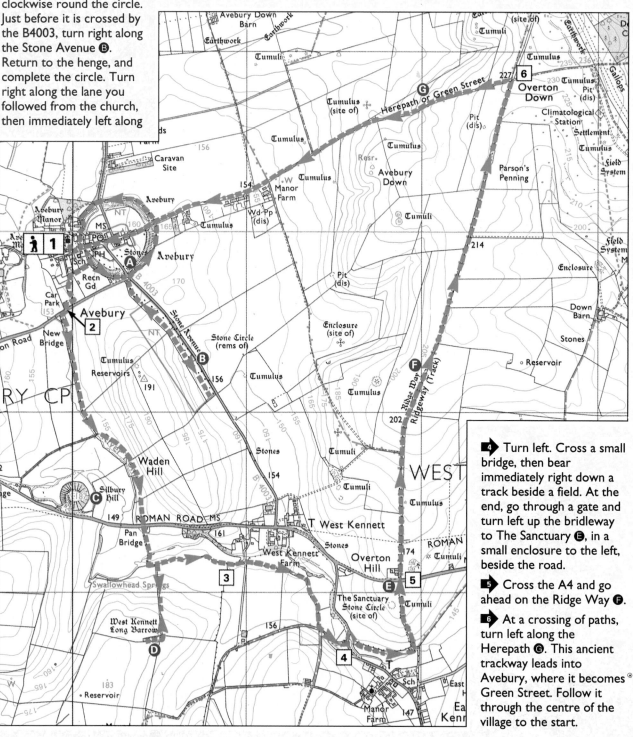

4 Turn left. Cross a small bridge, then bear immediately right down a track beside a field. At the end, go through a gate and turn left up the bridleway to The Sanctuary **E**, in a small enclosure to the left, beside the road.

5 Cross the A4 and go ahead on the Ridge Way **F**.

6 At a crossing of paths, turn left along the Herepath **G**. This ancient trackway leads into Avebury, where it becomes Green Street. Follow it through the centre of the village to the start.

from several miles away and hauled down ancient tracks to be set into four circles within the henge.

The largest stone, 'The Devil's Chair', is 23 feet (7m) long and weighs over 20 tons. An obelisk 18 feet (5.4m) high was set like the pin of a sundial within the southern circle; at the centre of the northern sector, a 'cove' was created from three enormous megaliths.

An avenue **B** of paired stones was constructed next, running southwards from the circles. Each pair consisted of a lozenge-shaped and a pillar-shaped stone, and some

◄*The distinctive outline of man-made Silbury Hill dominates the horizon ahead on the way south from Avebury.*

begins, the Norman font bears a carving of a Bishop who is stabbing one of a pair of winged serpents in the head with his crozier.

The standing stones are called 'sarsens', a corruption of 'saracen', meaning non-Christian. A concerted effort was made to remove these pagan survivals towards the end of the Middle Ages. Many of them were toppled into pits and buried.

The stone circles **A** predate Stonehenge by at least 500 years; many of the latter's stones came from this area. Both centres were built over several generations in the transitional period between the Stone and Bronze Age by people who lived close to the henges. Their only tools were stone axes,

▼*The impressive entrance to the five-chambered tombs of West Kennet Long Barrow, which may be 5,500 years old.*

deer-antler picks, blade-bone shovels, wicker carrying-baskets, leather ropes, and logs to lever or roll the massive stones.

They began by digging a circular ditch with high banks, 4,439 feet (1,353m) in circumference and 60 feet (18m) high. Grey-wethers, flat stones that from a distance resemble recumbent sheep, were selected

Nature Walk

ANTHILLS These domes belong to yellow field ants. Their soft, crumbly tops harden when the hill is deserted.

UFFINGTON WHITE HORSE Many decorative figures — some of which are very ancient — have been carved out of the chalky hillsides.

▲*The alternate pillar and lozenge stones along the Stone Avenue are believed to represent male and female principles.*

archaeologists believe that they symbolize male and female.

The route south goes along the River Kennet, past an even older construction than the stone circles and avenues. The 130-foot (39-m) mound known as Silbury Hill **C** is larger than many of the pyramids of Egypt. It would have taken 700 labourers 10 years to complete.

On the other side of the A4, which follows the course of a Roman road at this point, is West Kennet Long Barrow **D**. About 330 feet (100m) long, it is the second largest barrow in Britain, and is 1,000 years older than the other monuments around. The stone chambers inside contained bones from people crippled by arthritis.

Avebury's Saviour

The Avebury we see today would not have existed without the late Alexander Keiller. This Scot from the famous Dundee marmalade family gave his personal fortune and the most active years of his life to restoring what he saw as Britain's most important archaeological site.

Impressed by Stukeley's book on Avebury, then thought to be very

Alexander Keiller and his workmen erect an obelisk to mark the site of a vanished stone in West Kennet Avenue, Avebury.

eccentric, Keiller started excavating in the area in the mid-1920s, buying up land even where no trace of ancient monuments remained above the soil.

He helped prevent the building of a planned Marconi wireless station and tower, and slowly acquired the land on which ancient Avebury stood. Most of the stones seen today were located underground by his skilled teams — some lay as much as 8 feet (2.8m) deep — and were carefully raised in their former positions, where most of them had not been seen for centuries.

Keiller set up a museum in Avebury, where he exhibited and explained local discoveries, and used his wealth to fund a research institute. His description of Avebury between the wars reveals how bad things had become, with 'conditions of indescribable squalor and

neglect prevailing over most of the area ... a tangle of rusty pig-wire ... accumulations to a depth of nearly 3 feet [1m] of old tins and broken bottles...to say nothing of the refuse heaps which filled the ditch almost flush with its edges'.

Nevertheless, he embarked enthusiastically on the task of setting right 'the outstanding archaeological disgrace of Britain', and was only stopped by the outbreak of war in 1939. Ill health later prevented him from carrying on with his planned work. However, concrete pillars mark the sites where his teams were certain that buried stones were lying, or where sarsens had been destroyed.

Alexander Keiller died in 1955, and as a final act of goodwill left all the land he had acquired to the National Trust, which, he hoped, would complete the restoration. As yet, his dream remains unfulfilled.

▲*Groups of tumuli abound on the hills high above Avebury. The ancient track known as the Ridge Way (right), now a long-distance path, links Avebury with other prehistoric sites along the Downs.*

Curiously, the only complete skeleton found came from a man who was placed by the entrance before the chambers were sealed around 2000BC. This was after the completion of the stone circles at Avebury, when a new tradition of round barrow burials began. His death may have been sacrificial; an arrowhead was found in his neck.

Further along is The Sanctuary ❸, which was the end of the Stone Avenue from Avebury as well as the head of Stukeley's serpent. A

circular hut ringed by stones stood on this hilltop site. A large number of human bones have been found here, in what was perhaps a communal burial ground.

TIMELESS LANDSCAPE

From The Sanctuary, the route heads north along the Ridge Way ❺, a track some 5-6,000 years old. A steady climb, marked by tumuli, takes you onto the downs, where

larks rise over a timeless landscape of pastures and crop fields. There are good views away to the left over Avebury and Silbury.

Look north from the summit of Overton Down towards Monkton Down, or east to Fyfield Down, and you should see some grey-wethers. The return to Avebury follows the Herepath ❻, the ancient track along which the sarsens that made up the four stone circles were hauled.

AROUND THE STONES

40

WILTSHIRE

hostel attached to Amesbury Abbey.

The Abbey Church of St Mary and St Melor Ⓐ dates from the 12th century, although the majority of the building can be traced to the 13th century. Although long known as the 'Abbey Church', its links with the monastic house are not clear.

The first abbey, variously recorded as Ambrosbury, Ambresbury or

◀ *The full story behind the construction of the massive Stonehenge may never be known. Water mint (inset) grows near the stream you cross earlier on the route, and has a very pleasant smell.*

FACT FILE

✳ Amesbury, 7 miles (11.2km) north of Salisbury, off the A303

⌸ Pathfinders 1221 (SU 04/14) and 1241 (SU 03/13), grid reference SU 155414

miles 0 1 2 3 4 5 6 7 8 9 10 miles
kms 0 1 2 3 4 5 6 7 8 9 10 11 12 13 14 15 kms

◔ Allow at least 4 hours

▬ Mostly lanes and good, dry footpaths; one stretch, near Normanton, can be muddy and overgrown. Some long, but not steep climbs

🅿 Free car park in Amesbury centre (3 hours only Mon-Sat); unrestricted free car park at recreation ground (on route)

🆃 Amesbury is served by Wiltshire and Dorset Buses, Tel. (01722) 336855

▦ Several pubs and cafés in Amesbury. Refreshment kiosk at Stonehenge

🆆🅲 At Amesbury's central car park and at Stonehenge car park

⌂ Stonehenge (English Heritage) open daily: Tel. (01980) 623108 or 625368, fax (01980) 623465 for times; (admission charge)

🅸 Tourist information in Amesbury, Tel. (01980) 622833 or 623255

Approaching a famous ancient site through varied countryside

Few monuments in the world can equal the awe-inspiring grandeur of Stonehenge. Its isolated position on Salisbury Plain is emphasized by approaching it via the surrounding downland rather than the road. The centuries seem to fall away as you cross the wind-swept terrain, which is dotted with barrows and ancient earthworks.

The walk begins in the more cosy setting of Amesbury, an attractive town in a loop of the Avon Valley. Its numerous inns include The Bell — an old coaching inn from the days when people travelled by stage-coach to Salisbury along the Amesbury 'turnpike' — and The George, which dates back over 500 years to when it was a pilgrims'

121

Amblesberie, was founded in AD980 by Queen Ethelfrida, in penance for her part in the murder of her son-in-law, Edward the Martyr, at Corfe Castle. Arthurian legend suggests that an even earlier abbey existed, and that it was connected with Queen Guinevere.

By the 12th century, the nuns had become corrupt; Henry II turned them all out and replaced them with a more disciplined set. After the Dissolution of the Monasteries, the convent was demolished and a new mansion, designed by Inigo Jones, was built on the site.

GAY'S CAVE

There, the Duchess of Queensbury is alleged to have encouraged John Gay to write *The Beggar's Opera*, in 1728. A cave in the grounds, known as Gay's Cave, is where he is supposed to have worked.

◄ *The handsome Queensberry Bridge, built in 1775, spans the peaceful River Avon, which is enjoyed by waterbirds.*

The present Amesbury Abbey **B** was rebuilt in 1840 and is a private nursing home. The fine mansion, set in a park, can be glimpsed through the imposing stone entrance pillars next to the church.

The route crosses a footbridge over the River Avon alongside the Queensberry Bridge of 1775, then goes over the downs. Ahead there is a tumulus beside a chalk pit gouged from the hillside. Horizontal layers of black flint, such as was used for arrowheads by Neolithic man, can be distinguished in the chalk.

You follow a stream, then recross the Avon. Many species of water-loving plant flourish in the damp woodland here. You may spot the aromatic water mint, comfrey, water parsnip and marsh woundwort. The waterside is lined with the

THE WALK

AMESBURY – STONEHENGE

The walk starts in the main car park in Amesbury.

➤ Leave by the path to the left of the toilets, and turn right into Salisbury Street, passing the Bell Hotel on your right. Turn left into Church Street, and walk past the Abbey Church **A** and the entrance

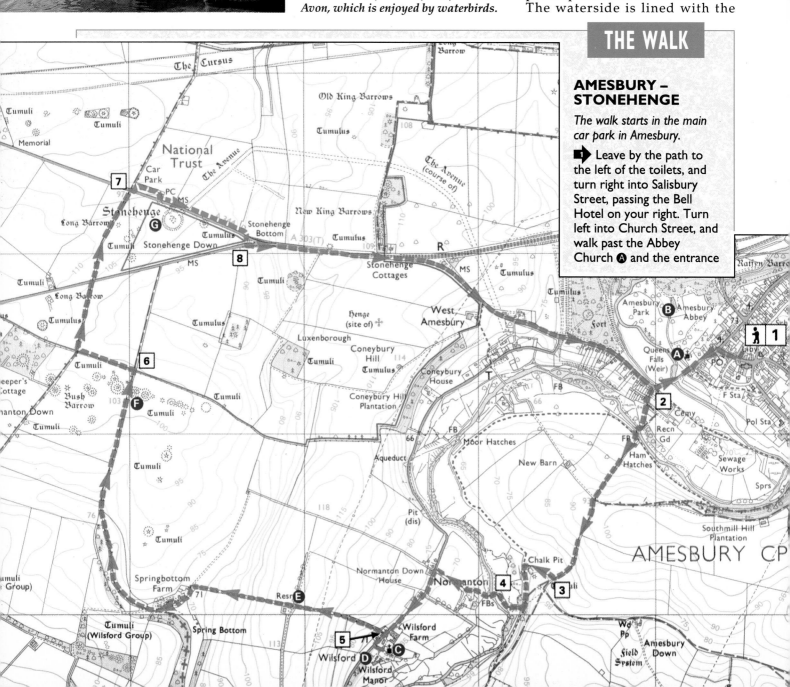

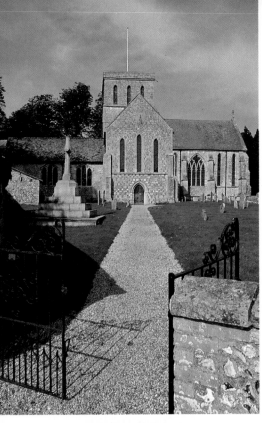

◄Amesbury's sturdy Abbey Church, dedicated to St Mary and St Melor, dates mostly from the 13th century.

renovated by Giles Loder, who faithfully copied the Early English style. The most interesting modern feature is a memorial by Eric Gill (1882-1940). This sculptor, wood engraver and typographer was the notorious focal figure of a series of 'Arts and Crafts' communities.

LOCAL COLOUR

The churchyard contains several graves of members of the Tennant family, a clue to the colourful past of neighbouring Wilsford Manor **D**, which is privately owned. The house, visible through the gateway, is in 17th-century style, with flint and stone chequerwork, gables and mullioned windows. It was actually built in 1903, on the site of a medieval manor, for Edward Tennant, the first Baron Glenconner, and his wife, Pamela Wyndham.

Their son, Stephen, was one of the 20th century's more eccentric characters. Wilsford Manor, where he spent his later years lying in 'decorative reclusion' among his sea-shells, jewels and polar bear skins, achieved nationwide fame when its contents were auctioned after his death in 1987. Newspapers

▲The impressive neo-Classical entrance to Amesbury Abbey, which is now a nursing home. In this chalkpit (below), gouged from the hillside, bands of flint can just be made out.

colourful spikes of purple loose-strife, pink and white Himalayan balsam and great willowherb.

In the delightful hamlet of Wilsford is St Michael's Church **C**, set in a pretty churchyard, with roses growing around the porch. Part of the foundations are 12th century, and there are some Norman arches and some chevron moulding, but the majority of the building was completed in the 14th and 15th centuries. In 1852, it was completely

---

to Amesbury Abbey **B**. Continue across the River Avon to a junction.

2 Walk up Recreation Road. Just before the car park by the recreation ground, take the narrow lane right, down to the Avon. Cross two footbridges. Follow the path as it veers left to a path junction. Turn right towards Durnford. Continue ahead, following the blue bridleway waymark uphill then down, to a path junction.

3 Go through the gate and take the downhill path right. At the bottom, turn left at the yellow waymark and follow the path by the ditch and stream. Cross a

wooden footbridge on your right. The path curves right, through the wood, to a small bridge over the Avon.

4 Cross this and the next footbridge. Follow the footpath right of the fenced garden and thatched wall. Climb the stile and turn right along the drive to a road. Turn left and walk for ¼ mile (400m), to Wilsford. Turn left down a walled lane to see Wilsford's church **C** and manor **D**. Retrace your steps along the road to the three cottages on your left.

5 Take the lane between them, signposted to Springbottom Farm. Continue ahead, up to the

viewpoint **E**, then down, and round the left side of the farm buildings. The track widens and curves right to head uphill, between pastures. Stonehenge comes into view ahead.

6 Just beyond Normanton Barrows **F** (on either side of the path), you reach the National Trust boundary. Climb the NT stile on your left. With the fence on your left, walk to a junction with a wide track and turn right. Carefully cross the A303, and continue in the same direction, with Stonehenge **G** on your right.

7 Turn right on the A344, cross, and walk

through the car park on the left, to reach the entrance to the Stonehenge site (a tunnel goes back under the A344 to the monument). After visiting the site, continue along the pavement on the left (north) side of the A344 to the junction with the A303. Cross the A344, then the A303.

8 Turn left to walk uphill on the right-hand (south) side of the A303. Keep on the pavement to fork right into Amesbury, and continue to the junction with Recreation Road. Turn left, back over the bridge, to retrace your steps through Amesbury to the car park.

Stonehenge

Europe's most famous prehistoric centre has a long and complex history; its construction took place over a period of about 1,500 years. Archaeologists and treasure-hunters alike have so disturbed the site that the exact sequence of its development may never be known.

It is likely that the first earthwork, a circular bank and ditch, was dug in about 3000BC, in an area already well-populated by herders and farmers. The first circle of bluestones, brought from the Preseli Mountains of south-west Wales, was raised in around 2,000BC.

Later, the bluestones were rearranged and an additional circle of larger sarsens was built, some of which weigh as much as 45 tons. They were apparently hauled over Salisbury Plain from the Marlborough Downs, 25 miles (40km) away. The resulting

This 1815 print is a fanciful depiction of an unlikely Druidical ceremony at Stonehenge.

monument is a miracle of prehistoric engineering; it has been estimated that the task of haulage and stone-raising took over 1½ million man-hours. The temple was complete by 1550BC.

Many theories have evolved to explain the monument's history and purpose. Norman writers, for instance, speculated that it had been erected by Merlin, King Arthur's wizard; in medieval times the stones were believed to have healing properties. Stonehenge is popularly believed to

have been used for human sacrifices, though there is no evidence for this. The Slaughter Stone, the large block by the entrance to The Avenue, was named in recent times.

A great deal of evidence suggests Stonehenge was a giant astronomical almanac, able to predict eclipses and phases of the sun and moon; on Midsummer Day, for instance, the sun rises over the Heel Stone to cast its shadow over the central Altar Stone. The particular significance of this is uncertain, but the cycles of time and the seasons must have been important to an agricultural people.

▲*This simple, pillared arch at St Michael's Church, Wilsford is a classic example of Norman architecture.*

retold Stephen's fascinatingly frivolous life. Wilsford Manor was host, in its heyday, to the Mitfords, the Sitwells and the Bloomsbury set.

A refreshing climb up the downs is rewarded with a first view of Stonehenge. From the viewpoint ❺, the path descends to skirt Spring-bottom Farm then turns up towards Salisbury Plain and Stonehenge. The

Bronze Age bowl and disc barrows ❻ on either side of the path include the famous Bush Barrow, visible at the far left of the group. In 1808, excavators found a skeleton buried with grave goods including gold lozenges (symbols of wealth), a belt hook, a bronze axe, a spearhead and a wooden dagger handle with a zigzag pattern of tiny gold pins.

STONEHENGE

You approach Stonehenge ❼ along a path known as the Druids' Lodge track. In fact, the Druids, a Celtic priesthood, came late to Stonehenge. They did not arrive much before 250BC, while the first monument on the site may date back to 2800BC.

The plain surrounding the henge contains a large number of other prehistoric features, some visible from the route back to Amesbury. The Avenue, whose parallel banks extend from the monument in approximate alignment with the dawn of the summer solstice, was probably a Bronze Age ceremonial approach to Stonehenge.

On the ridge to the north of Stonehenge is the Cursus; these

▶ *This delightful thatched cottage can be seen as you walk through Wilsford.*

parallel Neolithic ditches remain a mystery. King Barrows lie at right angles to the A303, and are part of a Bronze Age barrow cemetery. Vespasian's Camp, an overgrown Iron Age hill fort, lies between the A303 and the road into Amesbury.

Back at the main car park in Amesbury, you will notice a standing stone by the exit. This is the same type of blue stone, from Wales's Preseli Mountains, that was erected at Stonehenge. Placed there for charity in 1981, the stone neatly links the modern town and its fascinating prehistoric surroundings.

INDEX

PICTURE CREDITS